A COGNITIVE APPROACH TO

WORKING WITH OFFENDERS

William Davies

THIS BOOK IS THE PROPERTY OF:_____

ISBN No. 0 9520914 8 8

2nd Edition published by The APT Press
PO Box 3, Thurnby, Leicester LE7 9QN

CONTENTS

- Working in Groups
  - Possible benefits of groups therapy
  - Group therapy: A partial history
  - Research on Groups
  - Some varieties of group
  - Some general concepts particularly relevant to therapy in groups

MODULE FOUR: THE BROADER PERSPECTIVE

- Biological factors
- Environmental factors
- Social factors

REFERENCES

- Cognitive Approaches
- Group-work
- The Broader Perspective

INTRODUCTION

There are two questions:

- How effective is a Cognitive approach, with offending?

- How well can you learn to apply a Cognitive approach, by means of a distance learning programme?

How relevant is a Cognitive approach, with offending? One answer is that it is difficult to see how it could fail to be relevant. What we are talking about, after all, is how the way we view ourselves and the world, the way we think, and what 'rules' we have for ourselves and others, effects our feelings and behaviour To contend that our thinking style has no effect on behaviour would be radical to the point of incredulity. At another level, research studies, such as those of Novaco, Meichenbaum, provide a conventional scientific demonstration of its effectiveness. Personally, I am happy simply to see its efficacy at first hand.

On the other hand, it is not the *only* relevant factor in offending. We look at some of the other factors in component 4, the Broader Context. I have included that section not just because it has some useful information in it, but also as an antidote to a tendency that is difficult to resist when reading about cognitive approaches, namely that they are *the* answer. Naturally I am an advocate of a cognitive approach, but even so it would be an error to imagine that it cures all ills.

And how much can you learn from a distance learning programme? This depends on you. If you do all the exercises, you can learn an astonishing amount of relevant material that you can properly apply. If you skip the exercises and just go looking for so-called 'meat' then it will be much less useful. I have tried to make both text and exercises interesting to read and do, so I hope you do enjoy them and take time over them. If you do that, then I can see no reason at all why you should not have all you need to add a very sound cognitive dimension to your therapy. If you use no other approaches with your clients, then that will make you a cognitive therapist. However, I hope you do use all your current skills as well as cognitive approaches: as Paul Gilbert says "it doesn't do to be a one-club golfer."

This programme is in 4 modules:

MODULE ONE: WHAT IS A COGNITIVE APPROACH?

- the key concepts in a cognitive approach.

MODULE TWO: TECHNIQUES

- the techniques implied by those concepts.

MODULE THREE: MAKING IT WORK

- techniques are necessary, but not sufficient.

MODULE FOUR: THE BROADER PERSPECTIVE

- cognitive approaches are important, but not the whole story

In writing this programme I have had in mind the following readership:
Probation Officers, people working in Special Hospitals, Secure Units and Prisons.
I hope it is readable by people from a range of backgrounds. I have endeavoured to avoid any jargon which is specific to my own background as a psychologist, whilst endeavouring to be faithful to the concepts we discuss.

I hope that you enjoy completing this programme and that you and your clients benefit from it.

William Davies,
Thurnby

MODULE ONE:

WHAT IS A COGNITIVE APPROACH?

AIMS:

To develop a clear understanding of what is - and is not - a cognitive approach to offending, including:

- familiarity with *the cognitive model.*

- familiarity with short and long term *dysfunctional thinking.*

- familiarity with factors which, whilst not defining characteristics of the cognitive approach, *are generally associated with it.*

- familiarity with some *historical background* to the cognitive approach.

CHAPTER 1.1

WHAT IS A COGNITIVE APPROACH?

Now is probably as good a time as any for you to make your mark on this book, so let us start with an exercise. The cognitive approach, like many approaches, has its fair share of misconceptions associated with it, so this exercise is meant to help you sort out just what you currently believe the cognitive approach to be. I suggest you make an attempt at it even if you feel you have no idea what the answer is, or, alternatively, are quite sure you know already.

EXERCISE

What is a cognitive approach to offending? Include if possible

- What you believe to be 'the defining characteristics' of the approach

- Any factors you believe are generally associated with the cognitive approach, and

- Any techniques or ways of analysing material which are specifically *excluded* when using this approach.

Please do not move on until you have completed this exercise.

_____

_____

_____

_____

_____

_____

_____

_____

DISCUSSION OF EXERCISE

You might have written something like the following:

Defining characteristics:

- Hypothesizes that clients' thinking styles are an important factor in their behaviour (in this case their offending) and therefore concentrates on identifying and changing those thinking styles.

- Also stresses the importance of thinking styles in influencing how we feel (as well as behave).

- Is based on the cognitive model; ie a model which explains how behaviour and emotions are influenced by thinking style, and also how our individual thinking styles come about.

Factors generally associated with a cognitive approach

- Generally, interventions will be time-limited - say 10 sessions for example.

- The therapist and client will usually form 'a collaborative alliance', ie be working together on the offending. The therapist will not be 'berating' the client or acting as an 'expert'.

- Therapist and client will probably be agreeing 'homework assignments' for the client to do outside of sessions.

- Therapist will probably be using guided discovery or Socratic dialogue as a major tool.

- Therapist will probably have highly developed counselling skills and form a good relationship with the client.

Specifically excluded would be:

- Any significant consideration of the clients' unconscious processes .

- Any adventurous 'interpretations' of the clients' actions. However, this would not exclude an objective analysis of the function of those actions.

If what you have written looks like the above, congratulations. Not only do you have an extensive knowledge of cognitive approaches, you also have exemplary handwriting.

FURTHER INFORMATION RELATING TO EXERCISE

The Cognitive approach to helping offenders hinges on the realisation that the way we think influences our feelings and our behaviour. This is not a new realisation, it certainly goes back thousands of years, to the Greeks and beyond, but is one which has been adopted with increasing enthusiasm over the last few years in the U.K.

So, for example:

- If a man has his elbow jogged in a bar, spilling beer all over himself, it is important whether he thinks

    - *that was just an accident - it could have happened to anybody,* or

    - *that guy's trying to show me up - I'll teach him a lesson.*

    Plainly the latter may lead to more serious consequences for both parties.

Or:

- If a man is pushing his attentions on to a woman who rebuffs him, it is important whether he believes

    - *women are entitled to express who they want to spend time with,* or

    - *women are second class citizens - mainly for the convenience of men.*

    Again, the latter may lead to more serious consequences for both parties.

Over the centuries, most interest has been shown in applying what is now termed a 'cognitive' approach to *depression*. The much-quoted Greek philosopher, Epictetus, said that it is not events themselves which cause distress, but the view we take of them. Kant, in the 18th century, had not progressed much from that position when he said 'we cannot know of things in themselves, only our interpretation of them.' However, he also spoke of 'this handful of maxims which governs our lives.' Now, we would be more likely to talk about beliefs or rules rather than maxims.

In 1902, William James, usually thought of as the 'father of modern Psychology' wrote rather disparagingly of 'the religion of healthy-mindedness' and the idea that 'as you think, so shall you feel', believing that the popularity of such ideas then was beyond what was justified. Nevertheless, in 1948, Dale Carnegie wrote his excellent 'How to Stop Worrying and Start Living' which contained many valid ideas but was not in the mainstream of respectable academic psychology.

Especially from the '40s to the current day, psychologists and others have studied cognitive processes, especially concepts such as concentration, what we notice and don't notice, ('attention'), memory, retrieval (how we retrieve information stored in our memories) the effect our level of overall arousal has on these factors, and so on. While that was happening in the non-clinical world, the behavioural way of approaching things was gaining ground as far as a clinical approach (an approach to working with clients) was concerned. Various authors/clinicians applied cognitive concepts to clinical work. For example, Kelly (1955) generated personal construct theory which effectively applied cognitive findings into clinical work. Similarly, and importantly, Ellis produced Rational Emotive Therapy (1962), which looked directly at individuals' beliefs and endeavoured to work on them to achieve greater peace of mind for the client.

The word *'Cognitive'* means 'to do with knowing: perception, memory, beliefs, etc'
'*Cognitive Psychology'* is therefore the study of these processes, and
***Cognitive Therapy* is the application of the knowledge so gained, to help people in a clinical situation.**

Throughout the '70s, authors produced volumes which linked cognitive concepts into the prevailing Behavioural culture. Notable amongst these were Mahoney's *Cognition and Behaviour Modification* (1974), Beck's *Cognitive Therapy and the Emotional Disorders* (1976), Meichenbaum's (1977) *Cognitive Behaviour Modification*, and Beck et al's (1979) *Cognitive Therapy of Depression.*

It was probably the last of these which really set the world alight thanks to (a) again using the 'Cognitive Therapy' tag first used in 1976, and (b) being an excellent book. It was a text which made a very successful attempt to tell clinicians how they should approach the sometimes frustrating work of treating depressed people, and explained why the approach might work. Furthermore, whilst being in no way dogmatic, it also cited impressive evidence that it does work. Importantly, it was - and is - a cognitive-behavioural approach, clearly including behavioural methods as well as purely cognitive ones, in spite of its title.

'Cognitive Therapy' quickly became an important component in the treatment of depressed - and then anxious - people. Clinicians then looked at applying it to other areas, such as eating disorders, sexual problems, psychoses, and others. Offending behaviour is a natural front-runner for a cognitive approach, thanks to the very easily elicited 'automatic thoughts', beliefs/rules and views, that offenders sometimes display. In this area, the American psychologist Raymond Novaco has been at the forefront of applying cognitive strategies to anger management.

In summary, the cognitive approach hinges on several factors:

1. The realisation that *our thought processes affect our feelings and our behaviour.*

2. Clients' offending is sometimes exacerbated - or produced - by maladaptive thinking styles. For example

- in the way they interpret situations and events

- in their assumptions, beliefs and rules for behaviour

- in their views of themselves, the world and their future

3. The idea that we can identify such maladaptive thinking styles.

4. The idea that we can change clients' thinking style - or work with them to change it - and thereby reduce the likelihood of their offending.

Another way of looking at it, and a good one, is to say that when we are adopting a cognitive approach to working with offenders we have *the cognitive model* at the forefront of our minds. In some ways this sounds circular; it begs the question 'what is the cognitive model?' (We have already partly answered this question, earlier, but we answer it more fully later in the module.) In another sense it gets to the heart of the matter, because the cognitive approach is only partly about techniques, it is just as much about the way we conceptualise a person's offending.

CHAPTER 1.2

SHORT TERM DYSFUNCTIONAL THINKING

'AUTOMATIC THOUGHTS'

The concept of 'automatic thoughts' is an important one in a cognitive approach. It is also a very straightforward one: it simply refers to those thoughts that spring into our minds with no effort. So, in our example in the previous chapter, the man who had his elbow jogged had the automatic thought *"that guy's trying to show me up - I'll teach him a lesson."*

In that example, we can see how his automatic thoughts might well lead to him getting into a fight. However, the man who thought *"that was just an accident - it could happen to anybody"* was also displaying automatic thoughts, but this time they would tend to lead him away from a fight.

So, the first point is:

- **We all have automatic thoughts. There is nothing 'wrong' with having them - they are part of life.**

It is also true that:

- **Some people seem always to have automatic thoughts that lead them into trouble. What might be termed 'maladaptive' automatic thoughts.**

So the man who thought that he was being 'shown up' when he had his elbow jogged would probably think something similar if he had his toe trodden on, or someone got served before him in the bar, or he noticed another man looking at the woman he was with, or the bar staff accidentally gave him the wrong change, and so on.

And that:

- **People seem to have 'characteristic error patterns'. For example Jumping to Conclusions, or seeing things in All or None terms or Overgeneralising from one instance.**

In the 'jogged elbow' example both men were jumping to conclusions. There is actually no more evidence that it was an accident than for the idea that the guy was trying to show him up!

The net result of this automatic thinking is that it may lead to ***maladaptive interpretations of situations and events:*** interpretations that are against the interests of the offender or others.

Our task then, will be to mould the client's automatic thinking into *adaptive* **patterns. We will look at** *how* **to do this in modules two and three, but for the time being it is sufficient if we know** *what* **we are trying to achieve.**

We mentioned Jumping to Conclusions, and All or None thinking a moment ago, as patterns of automatic thinking which can be maladaptive. There are numerous such patterns, but the following are the most important ones:

1. **Selective Perception.** Where the client only seems to see one aspect of a situation and focuses on that to the exclusion of other relevant aspects.

2. **All or None thinking.** Refers to the tendency to think or evaluate events in extreme terms with no attention being paid to the 'middle ground'. For example, people are either 'for you or against you'.

3. **Jumping to Conclusions.** Drawing a conclusion when the evidence is lacking, is ambiguous, or even *contrary* to the conclusion.

4. **Magnification (or minimization).** Refers to the tendency to exaggerate the importance of a negative event (or to undervalue the importance of a positive one).

5. **Overgeneralisation.** Refers to the drawing of a general conclusion on the basis of a single incident.

6. **Mis-attribution.** Refers to the client mis-attributing the cause of an event - putting it down to something or someone other than what or who it really was.

Note:

These are only *examples* of maladaptive interpretations of situations and events, and individuals may develop their own idiosyncratic styles. Nevertheless, in practice, these do tend to be the major categories we come across. It is possible to see examples of all of these dysfunctional styles in offenders, and indeed in other groups. And in ourselves!

SOME EXAMPLES OF SHORT TERM DYSFUNCTIONAL THINKING IN OFFENDING BEHAVIOUR

Selective Perception

- *"I had to drive even though I was drunk ... it was an emergency"*

- *"I was evicted just because I owed £13"* (Where this is only one of the many reasons.)

All or None thinking.

- *"Mum's okay, but dad's a pain in the neck."*

- *"My previous probation officer was brilliant ... you're useless."*

Jumping to Conclusions.

- *"She is being friendly to me so she will go to bed with me."*

- *"He was looking at my girlfriend as a deliberate challenge to me."*

Magnification or Minimization.

- *"She deserved what she got; the cup of tea she made was stone cold."* (Magnifying the 'transgression', minimising the assault.)

- *"I know I've not been drunk this last week, but it's only because I've had no money."* (Ex-offender who would previously have stolen to buy alcohol, minimising current achievement.)

Overgeneralisation.

- "My mate got attacked by a black guy ... *they're all the same."*

- "John was let out over a year ago and is still looking for work - *ex-cons can never get a job."*

Mis-Attribution.

- *"The only reason she won't leave the club with me and come back to my place is because of her mates seeing - she fancies me really."*

- *"There's nothing the matter with me that giving up the booze wouldn't sort out"* (Attributing all problems to alcohol rather than any attitudes etc)

- *"The only reason he's closing up now is because I'm drinking here."*

EXERCISE

For each of the six common categories of dysfunctional thoughts, write down an example from your own experience. This might be a client, a friend, or yourself. *It need not be to do with offending.* Some examples have been filled in below, and you can also refer back to those on the previous page if you wish.

Selective Perception.

eg: I had a really good fortnight's holiday, but somehow <u>losing my suitcase on the flight home seems to have ruined it.</u>

_____

_____

All or None Thinking.

eg: I must be a <u>terrible</u> father; how could I do so little to help her with her homework.

_____

_____

Jumping to Conclusions.

eg: My friend Jo walked straight past me in the street yesterday, <u>I'm sure it's because Sam has been telling him about what I did two years ago.</u>

_____

_____

Magnification or Minimization.

eg: How on earth could I forget to mention Socrates when I was giving the talk to Probation Officers, that's ruined the whole thing.
(Maximising the omission, minimising the parts which went well.)

_____

_____

Overgeneralisation.

eg: I saw a client today who I've been seeing for over a year now, and he's still getting into fights. <u>I'm a hopeless therapist.</u>

_____

_____

Mis-attribution.

eg: It makes me really angry to see my wife putting on make-up when we go out, <u>to make herself attractive to other men.</u>
(If it is being done simply for her own self-esteem.)

_____

_____

15

EXERCISE

Now do the same exercise again, writing down examples from your own experience *which are to do with offending*. Try not to refer back to the previous pages unless you get stuck. Even if you feel this exercise is something of a repetition, do please complete it before moving on.

Selective Perception.

_____

_____

_____

All or None Thinking.

_____

_____

_____

Jumping to Conclusions.

_____

_____

_____

Magnification or Minimization.

_____

_____

_____

Overgeneralisation.

_____

_____

_____

Mis-attribution.

_____

_____

_____

THE DISCUSSION OF THIS EXERCISE
FOLLOWS ON THE NEXT PAGE

DISCUSSION OF EXERCISES

 **You probably found two things:**

1) When you were reading them, the categories of automatic thoughts seemed familiar and made sense.

2) When you came to try to produce your own examples of the six categories, this was quite difficult.

In a cognitive approach we will often agree a homework assignment with the client so that the work we do in session is continued into real life. Similarly there is an obvious homework assignment which will help here, namely to learn the 6 categories of automatic thought we have discussed, by heart.

Fortunately the initial letters of the six categories (Selective perception, All or none thinking, Jumping to conclusions, Magnification and minimisation, Overgeneralisation and Mis-attribution) form an acronym: SAJMOM. The downside of this is that it's not much of an acronym. But, if you are into jazz it is slightly reminiscent of Louis Armstrong's familiar name.

I would suggest you take the few minutes necessary to do the learning, not only of the six categories but also what they mean. You will find it pays off handsomely in that it makes it easier for you to spot such automatic thoughts when they occur in clients.

CHAPTER 1.3

LONG TERM DYSFUNCTIONAL THINKING:

MALADAPTIVE BELIEFS & RULES

In chapter two we looked at automatic thoughts, thoughts which appear 'from nowhere.' Triggered by a particular event, they may lead to a person mis-perceiving that event. They may be relatively transitory thoughts which sometimes may disappear as quickly as they came.

The next level down, in our thinking, is beliefs and rules. These are beliefs and rules about

- *How the world operates - or should operate*

- *How others behave - or should behave*

- *How we should behave.*

The kind of beliefs and rules we have can have a big bearing on how we feel, and it is easy to see why. For example:

- If we believe: *I should always do my best*

we will be repeatedly disappointed and dejected with ourselves when evidence comes tumbling in about one thing after another in which we have not done our best. *We cannot do our best at everything.*

- If we believe: *My value depends on what others think of me*

we will probably be anxious about the impression that we are creating on others, may alter our opinions to suit who we are talking to, and might be deeply depressed if we are rejected.

- If we believe: *I must succeed at everything I do*

then we may generate a lot of success for ourselves. But when confronted with failure we may be disappointed, anxious and depressed out of proportion to the event.

- If we believe: *If I do everything he wants he should love me*

we may become frustrated, bitter, disappointed or angry if this turns out not to be the case.

- If we believe: *I cannot be happy without her love*

  we may feel that life is not worth living if she rejects us.

So it is easy to see how such beliefs and rules can have very far reaching effects on our emotional well-being and - in the case of the last one - on our life expectancy. In the U.K. there is some convincing evidence that relationship break-ups are the biggest cause of people taking their own lives.

It is also possible to see how these beliefs and rules are much more permanent structures than automatic thoughts. The ideas *'I must always do my best'* or *'my worth depends on what other people think of me'* are not ones that flit across the mind. They recur time and again; they are inclined to be permanent.

Other beliefs, such as *'if I do everything he wants he should love me'* sound temporary but are not. It sounds as though there is a specific, possibly temporary, 'he' to whom this applies. And there probably is. However, we usually find that the same misconception about how people operate will re-appear with the next 'he' too. It is the misconception which is the problem, not the person who is the object of it.

The last belief we listed - *I cannot be happy without her love* - could also be thought of as an automatic thought. But I list it as a belief because it can be so strong, enduring and devastating that it feels as though it should have the right to be considered such. In truth it represents something of a grey area between automatic thought and belief.

So what does all this have to do with offending? Precious little as yet; we are just limbering up, getting used to the idea that our thinking style - our beliefs and rules in this case - can have a far-reaching effect on our emotions and behaviour.

In the next exercise we look at some beliefs which can be observed in some offenders, and the results that such beliefs can have.

EXERCISE

Below are listed some beliefs which have been observed in some offenders. In the first three the possible results of such beliefs have also been described. Read through these, then go on to the remainder and complete the 'possible result' section.

1. When women say No they don't really mean it.
   Possible result: Arguments, aggression, possible rape

2. Violence is the only way of getting what you want.
   Possible result: Repeated acts of violence, assaults.

3. Doing things legitimately gets you nowhere.
   Possible result: Long term involvement in underworld subculture.

4. Children are as capable as anyone else at deciding what they want to do.

   • Possible result: _____

5. A physical relationship with your own child is alright so long as it's a loving one.

   • Possible result: _____

6. Children know when they're being provocative.

   • Possible result: _____

7. If you don't stand up for yourself you will be pushed around.

   • Possible result: _____

8. It is dangerous to trust other people.

   • Possible result: _____

9. A good fight clears the air.

   • Possible result: _____

10. If people don't lock their property it's their fault if it's stolen.

   • Possible result: _____

DISCUSSION OF EXERCISE

Below are some possible answers. They are not the only ones of course, and most are self-evident. Even so, you may wish to compare them with what you have written.

1. When women say No they don't really mean it.
Possible result: Arguments, aggression, possible rape

2. Violence is the only way of getting what you want.
Possible result: Repeated acts of violence, assaults.

3. Doing things legitimately gets you nowhere.
Possible result: Long term involvement in underworld subculture.

4. Children are as capable as anyone else at deciding what they want to do.

   • Possible result: Persuading a child into a physical relationship

5. A physical relationship with your own child is alright so long as it's a loving one.

   • Possible result: Seducing son / daughter into a physical relationship as a misguided development of affection

6. Children know when they're being provocative.

   • Possible result: Mis-perception of child's play and as an 'invitation' to sexual contact.

7. If you don't stand up for yourself you will be pushed around.

   • Possible result: Over-aggressive behaviour

8. It is dangerous to trust other people.

   • Possible result: Social withdrawal and suspicion of others

9. A good fight clears the air.

   • Possible result: Frequent fights and loss of friendships

10. If people don't lock their property it's their fault if it's stolen.
   • Possible result: Involvement in repeated (petty?) thefts.

21

EXERCISE

Think about offenders you have seen, and note down beliefs or rules they have exhibited which may have underpinned their offending

eg: <u>Violence is the only way of getting what you want.</u>

1 _____

2 _____

3 _____

EXERCISE

Review the three beliefs / rules you have written above, plus the 10 in exercise 3.1 and put an asterisk * by the side of the *four* you consider to be the most important ones; the ones you can most closely link to offending or are most widespread in offenders you have seen.

Hopefully this chapter and its associated exercises have made apparent the link between beliefs / rules, and some offending. What it has not done is to show how such beliefs can be changed. We will examine that in Modules Two and Three. Module One aims simply to introduce the key concepts.

CHAPTER 1.4

THE COGNITIVE MODEL

In chapter 1, when we were discussing what a Cognitive Approach entailed, we said that it necessitated an understanding of the Cognitive Model. Indeed, right at the beginning of this module, the first bullet-point of the Aims was 'to develop a familiarity with the Cognitive Model.'

Well here it is. At least, here it is on the next page.

You will see that it was not really possible to introduce it earlier because we need a knowledge of short and long term dysfunctional thinking to make much sense of the model.

What the model purports to do is to explain how early experience leads to long term dysfunctional thinking, which predisposes the individual concerned to produce dysfunctional automatic thoughts, *given the right situation*. In turn, those automatic thoughts lead to the offending we observe, as we saw in chapter 2.

AN EXAMPLE OF THE COGNITIVE MODEL AS APPLIED TO ANGER CONTROL PROBLEMS

Early Experience

- Violent parent(s)

- Picked on / bullied

- Rejected / abused for small misdemeanours

Dysfunctional Beliefs and Rules

- Others are aggressive, competitive, over-bearing

- The world is a tough place / They are out to get you

- You have to show you're tough or people take advantage

- Those you trust abuse it (and you)

- Violence is the only way of getting what you want

Key Incident

- Elbow jogged in pub

Negative Automatic Thoughts

- He's trying to show me up

- People will expect me to respond

- People will think I'm scared if I don't respond

- If I don't respond others will take advantage of me too

Response

- **Emotional** Anger, fear

- **Behavioural:** Aggression, maybe violence

- **Cognitive:** Racing mind, inability to think clearly, impaired judgement

- **Physical:** Adrenalin surge, hyper-arousal

AN EXAMPLE OF THE COGNITIVE MODEL AS APPLIED TO A SEX-OFFENDER

Early Experience

- Father dominated mother.

- Treated in a preferential way to sister.

Dysfunctional Beliefs and Rules

- Men are superior to women.

- Women are here to serve the needs of men.

- Women should act the way I want them to.

Key Incident

- Made fun of / humiliated by potential partner.

Negative Automatic Thoughts

- She's 'out of order'.

- I need to teach her a lesson.

- I need to prove I'm not inadequate.

Response

- **Emotional:** Anger, humiliation.

- **Behavioural:** Aggression, maybe violence, maybe sex attack.

- **Cognitive:** Racing mind, inability to think clearly, impaired judgement

- **Physical:** Adrenalin surge, hyper-arousal

EXERCISE

AN EXAMPLE OF THE COGNITIVE MODEL

Think back over a client you have seen in the past, or are seeing currently, and attempt to fill in the blanks below, in much the same way as the examples on the two previous pages. The two examples both involved aggression in various forms. Your client here may do, or may have a quite different offending history, the choice is entirely yours. Feel free to 'experiment'; for example, if you change your mind about what you think your clients beliefs / rules are, cross them out and try again. Equally, if there are gaps in your knowledge, for example you don't know what the automatic thoughts are, or you are not sure what the early experience was, feel free to guess, placing a question mark after that entry, and - if you can - check it out later.

Early Experience

_____

_____

_____

Dysfunctional Beliefs and Rules

_____

_____

_____

Key Incident

_____

Negative Automatic Thoughts

_____

_____

_____

Response
- **Emotional:** _____
- **Behavioural:** _____
- **Cognitive:** _____
- **Physical:** _____

EXERCISE

AN EXAMPLE OF THE COGNITIVE MODEL

Try it again, with a different client. This should be quite an
enjoyable exercise because it often gives us an overall sense of
'what is going on' with a client. Don't feel that this is repetitive of the previous
page; the ability to conceptualise a client in terms of the cognitive model is a
fundamental skill in the cognitive approach, so doing it just twice is really very
little. However, we will examine it again, later on!

Early Experience

_____

_____

_____

Dysfunctional Beliefs and Rules

_____

_____

_____

Key Incident

_____

Negative Automatic Thoughts

_____

_____

_____

Response

- Emotional: _____

- Behavioural: _____

- Cognitive: _____

- Physical: _____

DISCUSSION OF EXERCISES

Hopefully you found those two exercises reasonably straightforward, providing you had sufficient information about your clients.

Having learned about short and long term dysfunctional thinking, the completion of the cognitive model form is easy so long as we have information about (a) the client's early experience and (b) what triggers an offence.

As we said on the previous page, being able to conceptualise our clients in terms of this cognitive model is a key skill in the cognitive approach. It is therefore a good idea to look back on exercises 4.1 and 4.2 from time to time, and maybe 'hone' them a little; maybe add information about the early experience, possibly change your mind about exactly what are your client's beliefs / rules, or just what the automatic thoughts are at the time of the offence, or whatever. Just generally to treat the cognitive model as your own, and to play around with your entries so that you eventually feel perfectly at home with each of the headings and can confidently write a cognitive model for almost any client you wish to.

Just in case you want to practise some more, here is a spare blank; photocopy it if you want.

THE COGNITIVE MODEL

PRACTICE SHEET

Early Experience

_____

_____

_____

Dysfunctional Beliefs and Rules

_____

_____

_____

Key Incident

_____

Negative Automatic Thoughts

_____

_____

_____

Response

- **Affective:** _____

- **Behavioural:** _____

- **Cognitive:** _____

- **Physical:** _____

CHAPTER 1.5

FACTORS GENERALLY ASSOCIATED WITH A COGNITIVE APPROACH

One of the striking aspects of Cognitive Approaches is that authors - and clinicians especially - have paid attention to how the therapy is conducted, as well as what it involves. Put another way, the manner - or process - of therapy, as well as its content

Given Lambert's (1989) review which demonstrates that the personal characteristics of the therapist are eight times more important than the techniques he or she is employing, and Goleman's (1985) finding that the relationship between therapist and client is a better predictor of success than the techniques employed, we are evidently well advised to pay special heed to these aspects - the manner of therapy. Conceivably, we should pay more attention to these than to the actual content of therapy (looking at the client's thinking processes).

On the next page I have listed some of the factors which have been shown to be important in therapy; they do not link directly with the research of either Goleman or Lambert. Interestingly, some of the factors listed can be very demanding on the therapist when working with some offenders. 'Unconditional Positive Regard' for example is one which some helpers find challenging when working with people who have committed offences which generate a strong negative emotional reaction in them.

In the list below we consider each in turn.

FACTORS GENERALLY ASSOCIATED WITH A COGNITIVE APPROACH:

1. **Counselling-type skills** such as empathy, warmth and genuineness, unconditional positive regard etc. The Cognitive approach, which is sometimes mis-represented as a directive or teaching approach, hinges on these. While it does have some elements of both of these, it is also clear that we must form a close alliance with the client if we are to stand any chance of eliciting the key thoughts which influence their offending.

2. **Collaboration** between therapist and client, with an open explicit relationship; two 'scientists' working together to resolve specific problems. Again, some people who work with offenders will find this aspect difficult, seeing it more as collusion than collaboration. Some indeed prefer to *confront the client* about their offending, rather than to *confront the offending behaviour with the client*. The former would be counter to a Cognitive approach, the latter in line with it..

3. **Clear goals**, usually - but not always - agreed between therapist and client. Once more this is one of the more difficult areas with offenders. While in mainstream clinical work people who are depressed, for example, are unmitigatedly clear about wishing to be less depressed, this is not so with some offenders who may be able to see clear advantages in, for example, continuing dishonesty, on with sex offences, or clear disadvantages in relinquishing violent behaviour.

4. **An Empirical approach**, whereby the client tests out his or her Automatic Thoughts, Beliefs, and Views.

5. **Homework tasks**, often related to 4, above.

6. **Time limited** in nature, covering a set number of sessions, each session of a predetermined length, with a clear structure.

7. **Immediacy**, emphasising the "here and now" rather than historical antecedents, unconscious processes, or 'interpretations'. We are, however, aware and responsive to the cognitive model, which refers back to previous events to explain current difficulties.

8. **Socratic dialogue, or guided discovery.** This is the use of questions as the main tool to highlight thinking styles and to change them. Hence we work to change the views and beliefs of clients by asking questions rather than persuading, cajoling, arguing or confronting a person.

CHAPTER 1.6

SOME HISTORICAL PERSPECTIVES

I want to finish this section with a short section on the history of cognitive approaches, not because it has special relevance for working with offenders, but rather to illustrate that the kind of ideas we are discussing are far from being new ones, and perhaps thereby to immunise us from rushing to and fro each new technique that appears and then disappears in cognitive approaches. The idea that the way we process information - our thinking style - affects the way we feel and behave has been around for thousands of years, so perhaps we can afford a certain humility about very specific techniques which seem to be revolutionary during a few years in the late 20th century!

1. Buddha maintained that the source of all human suffering was 'longing' and an attachment to the realm of the flesh. To escape from such pain, and to attain spiritual purity one had to turn away from such attachments and turn instead to wisdom. He went further and provided specific guide-lines for achieving this wisdom and spiritual purity.

2. Pythagoras (570-500BC) founded what became known as Rationalism, which asserts that thought is more powerful than the senses as a source of knowledge.

3. Socrates (469-399BC) noted for 'the Socratic Mission' ... a never ending search for truth, and a humility about current knowledge. We now refer to Socratic Dialogue as an asking of questions which prompt thought on a particular issue. Hence, Socrates (who was a Greek general at the time when Greece was involved in a series of punishing wars) might ask 'What is bravery?' to which the answer might be 'Bravery is where a man goes into battle knowing that he may well lose his life.' Socrates reply might be 'But supposing that man knew that he was suffering from a terminal illness which would result in a painful death, would he still be considered brave?' The answer is immaterial to some degree, the point is that it prompts thought on the issue and pushes the respondent to think of things in a way they had not done previously. More effective than simply asserting what Socrates considered to be bravery. (Such consideration did little good for Socrates stock from a state which wanted simple loyalty in difficult times, and he was eventually executed.)

4. Plato (427-347BC) saw the passions as unruly and animalistic, in line with Rationalism and contributing to the idea of Rational Supremacy, which asserts that reason can and should control everything. Epictetus (1st century AD) *'Men are disturbed not by things, but the view they take of them.*

5. Kant (18th century) *'We cannot know of things in themselves, only of our interpretations of them'* referring to what we call perceptions, and he also spoke of *'this handful of maxims which governs our lives'* which would equate with our beliefs and rules.

6. William James (1902) spoke somewhat disparagingly of 'the religion of healthy-mindedness' based on the idea 'as you think so shall you feel'. Seemingly he rather resented its then popularity.

7. Adler (1919) *'It is the meaning that is attached to events that determines behaviour.'* Hence Adlerian therapy looked at producing a more rewarding life for the patient by changing attitudes, values, goals and behaviour. The meaning of particular events for the client is still an important concept in the cognitive approach. Marketing people also use it: some cars have turbo-charged diesel engines and you occasionally see them badged as 'turbo' on the boot, rather than 'diesel'. Presumably this is to capitalise on the image of a 'turbo' being a sporty machine, whilst a diesel (to some) is a slow, noisy and smoky car. If the meaning of diesel slowly becomes 'smooth and ecologically sound' such a ploy would have to be dropped.

8. In the 1940s and '50s social learning theorists such as Miller and Dollard (1941), Rotter (1954) and Kelly (1955) discussed cognitive concepts such as attention, expectation, and personal constructs. At the same time, mainstream psychology was investigating our cognitive processes: how we remember things; why we pay attention to some things and not others; how it is that, if we are at a party and involved in a conversation we can still hear our own name if it crops up in an adjoining conversation which we thought we weren't listening to; our thought processes in other words. Our perception, storage and retrieval of information.

9. Bandura, in *Principles of Behaviour Modification* (1969) incorporated consideration of thought processes and previous experience into Behavioural thinking with concepts such as vicarious learning and modelling.

10. Ellis (1962) developed Rational Emotive Therapy, where patients' rules and assumptions about themselves and the world are deduced, then challenged, in order to help them cope more effectively with distress.

11. In the 1970s books such as (1974) Mahoney's *Cognition and Behaviour Modification,* Beck's (1976) *Cognitive Therapy and the Emotional Disorders,* Meichenbaum's (1977) *Cognitive Behaviour Modification,* and Beck et al's (1979) *Cognitive Therapy of Depression,* appeared.

COGNITIVE SELF-TEST, MODULE 1.

There is no need to write anything, just read the following questions and compose mental answers. Check back to the text if you wish. However, do ensure that you can answer them all *without checking back to the text* before moving on.

1
What are the *defining characteristics* of a cognitive approach to offending?

2
What factors are *generally associated with* a cognitive approach to offending?

3
Name one technique or way of analysing material which is specifically excluded from a cognitive approach to offending.

4
What are automatic thoughts?

5
If a man has his elbow jogged in a pub, spilling beer over himself, give two different automatic thoughts that might go through his mind.

6
We named six "characteristic" error patterns in automatic thoughts. The first one was selective perception. What are the other five?

7
Give an example from your own experience of mis- attribution.

8
Maladaptive automatic thoughts and maladaptive beliefs and rules are both examples of dysfunctional thinking. What is the main difference between the two of them?

9
Why might the "lock it or lose it" campaign, aimed at persuading people that it is their own fault if they don't lock their property and it is subsequently stolen, be counter-productive?

10
What underlying belief might lead to someone mis-perceiving a child's play as an invitation to sexual contact?

11
Name one underlying belief which might lead to over-aggressive behaviour.

12
What are the five stages involved in the cognitive model?

13
Give some examples of the kind of early experiences which might lead to the following dysfunctional beliefs:

"Other people are aggressive, competitive, overbearing ... "

"The world is a tough place and they are out to get you ... "

"You have to show you're tough or people take advantage ... "

"Those you trust abuse it and you ... "

"Violence is the only way of getting what you want."

14
There are good grounds for supposing that the factors generally associated with cognitive approaches (ie the way we go about therapy rather than the actual content of therapy) are quite crucial. Name six factors generally associated with the cognitive approach.

15
Because the term "cognitive therapy" was coined relatively recently, many people view a cognitive approach to human emotion and behaviour as a new one. Give three examples of how this approach has been operating - in one form or another - for thousands of years.

MODULE TWO

TECHNIQUES

AIMS:

To develop a familiarity with techniques available in a cognitive approach, specifically:

- Methods for identifying automatic thoughts, and changing them

- Methods for identifying beliefs and rules, and changing them

- Positive Self-Talk

- Benson's cognitive relaxation method

- Scheduling

- Record-Keeping

- Distraction

INTRODUCTION

In Module One we established that people's automatic thoughts - the way they perceive events - can affect how they will react to a situation. Similarly that their *beliefs and rules* about the world will also greatly affect their behaviour. Further, that both of these are fundamentally based in early experience.

In this Module we ask the question: *Supposing we now accept that the Cognitive Model of Offending has some relevance, what techniques might we use to decrease or eliminate a person's offending?*

This means we will be looking at

- Methods of identifying a person's automatic thoughts.

- Methods of changing them … identifying them is not enough.

- Methods of identifying beliefs and rules, and methods of changing them.

- Positive Self-Talk; establishing positive perceptions rather than simply eliminating negative ones.

- Benson's cognitive relaxation method.

- Helping clients to schedule specific activities through the week.

- Record-Keeping.

- Distraction.

Only one word of warning. Most of us find 'techniques' rather appealing, and sometimes people will misrepresent a Cognitive Approach as a 'technology' for intervening effectively. If ever we are tempted to think like that it is worth reminding ourselves of Lambert's 1989 finding that the characteristics of the therapist are 8 times more important than the techniques used, and Goleman's 1986 finding that the relationship between the therapist and client is a better predictor of outcome than is the technique used. In *Module 3* we look at meshing those findings with the knowledge of cognitive techniques we will acquire in this module. Put another way, *by the time you have studied this module, you should know the techniques involved in a cognitive approach to offending, but you may not know quite how you would use them.*

CHAPTER 2.1

METHODS FOR IDENTIFYING AUTOMATIC THOUGHTS.

What we are trying to do here is to uncover the automatic thoughts that the person has at the time of the offending. Sometimes these thoughts will vary according to the particular offence, but often we find that the person has a characteristic thinking style. For example one person may be inclined to *jump to conclusions*, another to exhibit *all or none thinking*, a third to *mis-attribute* things, and so on. In other words, different people may exhibit different ones of dysfunctional thinking styles summarised by the SAJMOM acronym.

Two things to remember however:

- Such thinking is not *always* dysfunctional. For example, most of us are inclined to jump to conclusions from time to time. This means we have to be pretty sure that the particular element of SAJMOM we have noticed is in fact relevant to the offending.

- The SAJMOM acronym gives us just six forms of short term dysfunctional thinking, and there are other categories as well. Indeed, although the SAJMOM categories are probably the most common, individuals will sometimes invent dysfunctional thinking styles which are idiosyncratic, specific to themselves.

It is also worth bearing in mind that we do not purport to explain all a person's offending by means of their automatic thoughts. We need to bear in mind a number of other factors, not least their beliefs and rules. We examine them in chapter 2.2.

So with these provisos, turn over for the main ways of identifying automatic thoughts.

MAJOR WAYS OF IDENTIFYING AUTOMATIC THOUGHTS

1. **By Interview**: listening carefully to what the client has to say, and gradually identifying any category of automatic thought which is repeatedly working against the interests of the client. It is clearly important to investigate what the person was thinking at the time of an offence. We rely on our interview skills here, but two points worthy of note:

- Concentrate on one specific offence rather than offending in general. Having talked about one specific offence, move on to talk about another, and so on, so that you gradually build up a picture of the person's usual thinking processes at the time of offending.

- One useful phrase, of many possible, is *'What went through your mind when ....*
    - *... he jogged your elbow in the bar'* or
    - *... she suggested that the two of you went out shoplifting'* or
    - *... you were play-fighting with her'* etc.

2. **Talking to 'significant others'** and inferring automatic thoughts from their accounts. For example, if our client assaults his or her domestic partner, that person may be a very good source of information. The sort of things that our client says at the time of the assault may be exactly the thoughts they are thinking at the time.

3. **The use of diary forms** such as the Be Your Own Best Friend form which is included in this programme later. Such forms can either be filled in by the client at or around the time of the offence, or when they are tempted to offend, or we can complete it with our client when we meet.

4. **Role-Play**, which is especially useful where the client says, for example: "I just can't remember what I was thinking ... I know I was very angry, but I can't remember what was going through my mind." Sometimes literally re-enacting the event in question will lead to the thoughts and images coming back too.

Note:
Some people tend to think in words, others mainly in pictures and images. This needs to be borne in mind, both in interview and in diary forms. For example, emphasising that they might describe a particular image which came to mind. Eg *"When she suggested we went out shop-lifting I straightaway had this picture of the two of us falling around laughing and feeling really good, the last time we went out like that."*

Tip:

When we listen to someone talking about their offending we can feel overwhelmed when they seem to display just about all the categories of dysfunctional automatic thoughts. One moment they may be jumping to conclusions, the next moment they may be showing all-or-none thinking, at a third time they may overgeneralise. Rather than being overwhelmed, or worse still simply telling the person about all the logical errors they are making, it is best if we can identify the category of automatic thinking which is at the forefront of causing the person's difficulties. Then we can help them work on this one problem and, if we sort it, reap manifold rewards.

For example, our man with the famously jogged elbow in the bar *jumped to the conclusion* that (a) someone was trying to show him up and that (b) his mates would deride him if he did not thump the person who jogged him. Well maybe he is in the habit of jumping to conclusions. If so, that is a much more circumscribed problem and probably one which is much more easily helped, than 'being aggressive'.

EXERCISE:

- Try to bring to mind an offender with whom you are currently working and who you would like to think about in this context.

- Then replay in your mind the most recent conversation you have had about the offending.

- Then ask yourself which of the six categories of dysfunctional thinking was most prevalent ... if there was one category of dysfunctional thinking you could eradicate at the touch of a button, which would it be?

- To help, the initial letters of the six categories are listed below; you might like to complete them before proceeding.
    - S......... ....
    - A.. .. ..
    - J...... .. ..
    - M............ (.. M...........)
    - O................
    - M..-...........

CHAPTER 2.2

METHODS FOR CHANGING AUTOMATIC THOUGHTS.

(This is a slightly long chapter, but it is as well if you get the best out of it because doing so will not only be powerful in its own right, it will also stand you in good stead when we come to look at changing beliefs and rules, later on.)

Plainly it is not sufficient simply to identify the automatic thoughts that put a person at risk of offending, we also need to change them. Just as identifying the cause of a car being dangerous to drive - for example that its brakes have failed - does not in itself make it a safer vehicle.

The general method for this, in the cognitive approach, is that of Socratic dialogue, also called guided discovery. This might be described as

- **The asking of questions which may give the client a new perspective on a situation.**

So, with our poor chap we keep going on about, the one who had his elbow jogged in the bar, and jumps to the conclusion that the other man was trying to make a fool of him, we might say

- "Could there be any other reason why he jogged your elbow?" Or,

- "Supposing a friend of yours had his elbow jogged in the bar, jumped to the conclusion that the guy did it deliberately, and was about to risk a few years in prison by smashing a beer mug in the bloke's face, what would you say to him?" Or,

- "What evidence do you have to back up what you say about this guy having jogged your elbow *deliberately? ... And is there any evidence to suggest that it might have not been deliberate?"* Or,

- "What were the advantages for you, in believing that the guy jogged your elbow deliberately? ... And were there any *dis*advantages?"

Or indeed any other questions that our ingenuity can summon up in order to possibly give the person another perspective on the situation. Hopefully a perspective which is closer to some objective reality, and certainly, again hopefully, one that is more adaptive.

You can see the trap with these questions, however. If we ask such questions in the wrong tone, or the wrong spirit, they can come across as 'smart', in which case the likelihood of making progress with our clients is going to be close to zero. This is one reason why the spirit of 'collaborative empiricism' - two equal experimenters investigating a hypothesis together - is a crucial one in the cognitive approach.

So the actual phraseology of the questions might turn out more like:

- "Let's have a look ... could there be any other reason why he jogged your elbow? ... exactly what happened?" Or,

- "Supposing a friend of yours had his elbow jogged in the bar, jumped to the conclusion that the guy did it deliberately, and was about to risk a few years in prison by smashing a beer mug in the bloke's face ... I wonder what might be the best thing to say to him?" Or,

- "Let's have a look what evidence there is to suggest that this guy jogged your elbow *deliberately? ... And let's have a look to see if there is any evidence to suggest that it might have not been deliberate?"* Or,

- "I wonder what advantages there were for you, in believing that the guy jogged your elbow deliberately? - What do you think? - And were there any *dis*advantages?"

Usually, though, the collaborative nature of the interaction is conveyed more by our *tone*, rather than anything we can write on paper. *Overall, we are trying to replace argument, confrontation, debate and persuasion, with guided discovery - the client reaching his or her own conclusions, usually through working with us on questions we pose.* Socratic dialogue, in other words.

So let's indulge in some Socratic dialogue on another SAJMOM dysfunctional thinking style, mis-attribution:

- *"There's nothing the matter with me that giving up the booze wouldn't sort out"* (Attributing all problems to alcohol rather than any attitudes etc)

We might say:

- "I wonder if there might be another way of looking at this ... what do you think?" Or
- "If a friend of yours kept getting into trouble with the law, and kept putting it down to the drink he was getting through, what would you say to him?" Or
- "Let's have a look at the evidence for what you've just said ... and now let's see if there's any evidence that would suggest some other explanation." Or

- "I wonder if there are any advantages for you in seeing it that way - let's have a look. And let's see if there are any disadvantages in seeing it like that."

Only rarely will single questions like these examples result in our client changing his or her perception of things. Much more often it will be the beginning of a genuine *Socratic dialogue* - or conversation - which *may* result in a change in perception. The important concept is that we and the offender are in this together, and trying things out together; there is a spirit of *collaborative empiricism*. After all, we always have to remember that although he or she may, for example, be jumping to conclusions, they may also be right. We therefore have a certain humility about alternatives that we jump to, no matter how sure we are at the time!

But how do we think of these questions? In two ways:

- First, there is no hurry, so we will sometimes mull over what a client has said between sessions, deciding which are the key thoughts to tackle and how we will go about doing it.

- Second, there are some guidelines, as follows:

- Ask what Alternative 'ways of looking at it' there are. After all, until a client has an alternative way of perceiving an event s/he may be very resistant to letting go of the current perception.

- Ask "Are you saying to yourself what a Friend would say to you?" Or, "Are you saying to yourself what you would say to a friend?"

- Ask "What is the Evidence in support of seeing things this way?" And then, "What is the evidence against seeing it this way?" It seems to be important to take the evidence this way round. Once clients have explained fully why they think the way they do, they are sometimes much more amenable to looking at the evidence for an alternative perception of the situation.

- Ask "What are the Advantages and Disadvantages of seeing things this way?" The idea here is that clients will be swayed by the fact that there are more disadvantages than advantages to the way they are thinking, and therefore be amenable to alternative perceptions. Sometimes, however, the balance can come as a shock to the *therapist*.

- This is not Socratic dialogue, **but clients will sometimes react well simply to having it pointed out that they are (eg) jumping to conclusions, or thinking in an all or none fashion, etc.**

EXERCISE

Below you will find, reprinted from Module 1, the 13 dysfunctional perceptions under the six SAJMOM categories of dysfunctional automatic thoughts. Choose two of the dysfunctional perceptions to change, using Socratic questioning. Fill them in on the next page, and then create 4 questions similar to those in the examples on the previous two pages.

Selective Perception
- *"I had to drive even though I was drunk ... it was an emergency"*

- *"I was evicted just because of £13"* (where this is only one of the many reasons.)

All or None thinking.
- *"Mum's okay, but dad's a pain in the neck."*

- *"My previous probation officer was brilliant ... you're useless."*

Jumping to Conclusions.
- *"She is being friendly to me so she will go to bed with me."*

- *"He was looking at my girlfriend as a deliberate challenge to me."*

Magnification or Minimization.
- *"She deserved what she got; the cup of tea she made was stone cold."* (Magnifying the 'transgression', minimising the assault.)

- *"I know I've not been drunk this last week, but it's only because I've had no money."* (Ex-offender who would previously have stolen to buy alcohol, minimising current achievement.)

Overgeneralisation.
- "My mate got attacked by a black guy ... *they're all the same.*"

- "John was let out over a year ago and is still looking for work - *ex-cons can never get a job.*"

Mis-Attribution.
- *"The only reason she won't leave the bar with me and come back to my place is because of her mates seeing - she fancies me really."*

- *"There's nothing the matter with me that giving up the booze wouldn't sort out"* (Attributing all problems to alcohol rather than any attitudes etc)

- *"The only reason he's closing up now is because I'm drinking here."*

TRIAL 1
Dysfunctional perception, chosen from opposite:

_____

_____

Socratic questions:
1) Alternative (see pages 6 & 7 for examples)

_____

_____

2) Friend (see pages 6 & 7 for examples)

_____

_____

3) Evidence for and against (see pages 6 & 7 for examples)

_____

_____

4) Advantages and Disadvantages of seeing it this way (see pages 6 & 7)

_____

_____

TRIAL 2:
Dysfunctional perception, chosen from opposite:

_____

_____

Socratic questions:
1) Alternative (see pages 6 & 7 for examples)

_____

_____

2) Friend (see pages 6 & 7 for examples)

_____

_____

3) Evidence for and against (see pages 6 & 7 for examples)

_____

_____

4) Advantages and Disadvantages of seeing it this way (see pages 6 & 7)

_____

_____

 **DISCUSSION OF EXERCISE**

Hopefully, what you have written may look something like the following, although you may have chosen different examples.

TRIAL 1

Dysfunctional perception, chosen from opposite:
"She deserved what she got; the cup of tea she made was stone cold."

Socratic questions:

1) Alternative (see pages 6 & 7 for examples)
   Do you think that there is any other way of looking at this?

2) Friend (see pages 6 & 7 for examples)
   Suppose you had a friend who had got himself into serious trouble with the law — was risking getting himself locked up maybe - on account of his wife giving him a cup of cold tea, what would you say to him?

3) Evidence for and against (see pages 6 & 7 for examples)
   Let's have a look at this. You're saying that if someone's wife brings them a cup of tea that isn't very hot, they deserve to get beaten up. Can you think of any other people who do that? ... Can you think of any people who would act differently?

4) Advantages and Disadvantages of seeing it this way (see pages 6 & 7)
   Let's have a look at this. You're saying that if someone's wife brings them a cup of tea that isn't very hot, they deserve to get beaten up. Let's have a look what advantages there are in seeing it this way. (Feels less guilty, can justify himself to people who challenge him, etc) ... And let's have a look if there are any disadvantages in seeing it this way. (Means that he doesn't look at other ways of behaving, may therefore keep getting into trouble. Will probably find it difficult to find a long-term partner, etc.)

Note: Examples such as this can severely test our collaborative attitude and we can find ourselves wishing to revert to what Transactional Analysis folk would call 'Parent' mode, strongly wishing to give the person a bad time regardless of whether or not this will lead to a reduction in offending, or possibly seeking to rationalise such a 'telling off' by insisting that it must surely lead to such a reduction. If we wish to practise a cognitive approach, however, we need to stay 'adult-adult'!

TRIAL 2:

Dysfunctional perception, chosen from opposite:
John was let out over a year ago and is still looking for work - *ex-cons can never get a*
job."

Socratic questions:
1) Alternative (see pages 6 & 7 for examples
Do you think there is any other way of looking at this? Is there any other explanation
for why he hasn't been able to find a job?

2) Friend (see pages 6 & 7 for examples)
Supposing a friend of yours had been in prison for a while and was having trouble
finding a job afterwards, even though he was capable of good work, what would you say
to him?

3) Evidence for and against (see pages 6 & 7 for examples)
So you're saying that people who have been in prison can never find a job afterwards.
Let's have a look to see what evidence there is that would back that up. (John hasn't
found a job, neither has Jim, etc) ... And let's have a look at what evidence there is that
would go against that. (Ken has found a job, even though he's been in prison, so it is
possible to find a job after a sentence, etc)

4) Advantages and Disadvantages of seeing it this way (see pages 6 & 7)
Let's have a look what advantages and disadvantages there are in seeing things this
way. Advantages first. (It lets you out of looking for a job - what's the point if ex-cons
can never get one; you can feel less guilty about having no job - it's not your fault,
it's the system.) And disadvantages. (It means you're never likely to find a job,
because you're not really looking for one; therefore you'll be more likely to end up
stealing and back in trouble again, etc)

OBSERVATIONS

1. These ways of changing dysfunctional automatic thoughts can be remembered
using the initial letters of Alternative, Friend, Evidence (for and against) and
Advantages / Disadvantages. This spells AFEAD, which at least *sounds like* the
old English 'Afeared', as in *"I was terribly afeared I would get into trouble."*

2 For any particular dysfunctional thought, one or two of the AFEAD questions
work quite well, others not so well. We have to choose our intervention
depending on what the thought is.

LINKING SOCRATIC QUESTIONS:

What do we do when the following happens?

Client: *"There's nothing the matter with me that giving up the booze wouldn't sort out"* (Attributing all problems to alcohol rather than any attitudes etc)

Us: *"If a friend of yours kept getting into trouble with the law, and kept putting it down to the drink he was getting through, what would you say to him?"*

Client: *"I'd tell him he's not drinking enough, probably."*

One possibility is to repeat the question in different words ('Broken Record' as it's called in assertiveness training), another is to follow up with different (Socratic) questions, and develop a *Socratic dialogue*. So it might go something like this:

Us: *"Is that what you'd really say?"*
Client: *"No, probably not."*
Us: *"Go on then, what would you really say?"*
Client: *"Drinking never helped anyone."*
Us: *"How do you mean?"*
Client: *"Well it doesn't does it ... not really."*
Us: *"What about for yourself, has it helped you?"*
Client: *"No, but I get into trouble anyway. It's just that I'm usually drunk."*
Us: *"Do you mean that sometimes when you get into trouble you're not drunk?"*
Client: *"Yes, sometimes."*
Us: *"So what is it about you that means you get into trouble, when some others don't?"*

Obviously some of our questions are rather better ones than others, and that is usually how it is. It is the last one that gets us properly on track for looking at what underlies this person's offending (apart from the alcohol consumption). Of course the reply to the last question may be a non-committal

"Well I'm just different from other people," in which case we persist with

"Different in what way," and so on, until we and our client both begin to see just what the difference is, just what it is that underlies the offending.

The general point is that one (Socratic) question is rarely enough; usually we have to link them into a Socratic dialogue or Socratic conversation. One **which may give the client a new perspective on a situation,** and will certainly allow both of us an exploration of the client's 'inner reality'.

Which of the following therapists would you rather be?

Therapist A: Asks 'shrewd' questions which eventually corner the client and apparently force him into the therapist's way of seeing things.

Therapist B: Has genuine curiosity about the way the client sees things, whether it is an adaptive way of seeing things, how his perceptual style might be modified to be more adaptive, and how he or she can work with the client to produce change.

Note:

You may by this stage be getting 'technique-blind', having now read about several techniques but without much talk of how this applies in a clinical setting. Not to worry, this is what we discuss in component 3. A point worth making now, however, is that homework tasks play a key role in this respect; ideas we simply discuss with the client are given real meaning when the individual tries to act on them outside the clinical situation. Our ability to persuade the person to do this is therefore important.

EXERCISE

Put your feet up (metaphorically if you want) for a couple of minutes and simply envisage having the kind of Socratic dialogue we have just described, with a person you are currently working with. Remember, we are not being smart, we are helping the person to explore their psychological terrain and, eventually, to produce a more fruitful landscape.

There is no need, but if you have any observations you want to record, here is the space to do so:

_____

_____

_____

_____

_____

CHAPTER 2.3

METHODS FOR IDENTIFYING BELIEFS / RULES

1. **By Interview**: listening carefully to what the client has to say, and gradually identifying beliefs and rules which are working against the interests of the client. We rely on our interview skills here. You may remember some of the beliefs / rules we mentioned in Module One. It is easy to see how some of these could become apparent in interview, so long as we are discussing the relevant areas. The following are examples:

   • Violence is the only way of getting what you want.

   • Doing things legitimately gets you nowhere.

   • If you don't stand up for yourself you will be pushed around.

   • It is dangerous to trust other people.

   With some of the others it is more difficult to see how they could possibly come up in general interview conversation. One would need to be much more focussed on the specific offending to stand a reasonable chance of unearthing them. Examples of these are :

   • When women say No they don't really mean it.

   • Children are as capable as anyone else at deciding what they want to do.

   • A physical relationship with your own child is alright so long as it's a loving one.

   • Children know when they're being provocative.

   • A good fight clears the air.

   • If people don't lock their property it's their fault if it's stolen.

   One of the traps with unearthing beliefs and rules is that we may find that the person has beliefs and rules which we strongly disagree with, and may believe are immoral, *but nevertheless are unrelated to his or her offending*. In that instance we may have to question ourselves very closely before deciding whether or not we are justified in attempting to change those beliefs and rules.

2. **Talking to 'significant others'** and inferring the client's beliefs and rules from what they say. These may become apparent in everyday interchanges between the two of them. Such a 'significant other' may therefore be an excellent source of clinically relevant information.

3. **The use of diary forms** such as the Be Your Own Best Friend form which is included in this programme later. Such forms can either be filled in by the client at or around the time of the offence, or when they are tempted to offend, or we can complete it with our client when we meet. In either case they may provide some very clear data.

4. **Role-Play**, which is especially useful where the client says, for example: "I just can't remember what I was thinking ... I know I was very angry, but I can't remember what was going through my mind." Sometimes literally re-enacting the event in question will lead to the thoughts and images coming back too.

5. **The downward arrow technique.** Where you respond to the client's initial general assertions with responses which funnel his responding downwards and into more specific thinking. For example:

Us: How did the offence come about?
Client: There wasn't really an offence
Us: So what happened in the incident that led to you being convicted?
Client: We went back to her flat, and things went on from there.
Us: Things went on from there?
Client: We went to bed.
Us: Was she agreeable to that?
Client: Yes, I think so.
Us: What made you think that?
Client: I just thought she was.
Us: What made you think that?
Client: She didn't put up much of a fight.
Us: But she put up some sort of fight?
Client: Yes, but *women always say No they don't really mean it.*

And this was virtually one of the examples of beliefs we mentioned earlier. In this particular case, it is difficult to be sure whether we have nicely funnelled downwards to a maladaptive belief, or whether we have simply 'cornered' the client into saying something he does not really mean, in order to save face. *For this reason it is important to develop a gentleness of technique.*

Other beliefs / rules which might be uncovered by a similar downward arrow procedure might include (from our list in module one):

- Children are as capable as anyone else at deciding what they want to do.

- A physical relationship with your own child is alright so long as it's a loving one.

- Children know when they're being provocative.

- A good fight clears the air.

- If people don't lock their property it's their fault if it's stolen.

There are plenty of others as well. Note any that occur to you, here, if you wish:

_____

_____

_____

_____

_____

CHAPTER 2.4

METHODS FOR CHANGING BELIEFS / RULES

Just as it is not sufficient simply to identify automatic thoughts that put a person at risk of offending, neither is it sufficient simply to merely identify maladaptive rules / beliefs. If our client possesses such beliefs or rules, we need to change them too.

As with changing automatic thoughts, the general method is that of Socratic dialogue, also called guided discovery: **The asking of questions which may give the client a new perspective on a situation.**

We generate the questions in just the same way as we did for automatic thoughts, namely by asking our client:

1. What **A**lternative beliefs / rules are there?

2. Are you saying to yourself what a **F**riend would say to you? Or, Are you saying to yourself what you would say to a friend?

3. What is the **E**vidence in support of this belief/rule? And then, What is the evidence against the belief/rule?

4. What are the **A**dvantages and **D**isadvantages of holding this belief / rule?

And the same comments about finding a user-friendly form of words for the questions we ask holds good here as well. In fact, for much of the time it really doesn't matter too much whether we conceptualise ourselves as challenging automatic thoughts or dysfunctional beliefs / rules.

However, there are two others which are specific to Beliefs/Rules, rather than NATs.

- *State clearly the belief which the client is acting on.*

    For example: "You *believe that there is only one way of getting what you want, and that's to thump someone, don't you?*

    Frequently the very absurdity of the belief will lead the client to generate a more adaptive one, eg:

    "No ... of course not. It's one way though.

    Again though, interchanges such as this highlight the importance of maintaining a robust and friendly *relationship*, without which the client would not feel 'open' enough to back-track at all.

- **The behavioural test. That is, you persuade the client to test out his belief / rule in real life.** For example:

"You believe that if you don't thump the person who accidentally spills beer over you, your friends will think you're soft and desert you."

"Well, yes, and they would too."

"Would you be prepared to test that out?"

And so on. From then on it is down to your powers of persuasion.

Note: In fact, this method also applies to changing dysfunctional automatic thoughts. In practice, however, it seems to be more useful in changing dysfunctional beliefs / rules.

Tip:

All these techniques hinge on a good relationship. No amount of clever questioning will persuade a person to 'put his neck on the line' as they would see it, unless they absolutely trust us. We have to remember that, with beliefs / rules more than with automatic thoughts, we are dealing with ideas which the person has carried around with them for years and may hold as absolute truths. The idea that these are not truths, but simply opinions which are open to testing, may be a very radical one indeed. Equally, we need to maintain our own humility in this respect: some people may be absolutely correct when they say their friends will desert them if they do not thump the accidental transgressor. It is a true behavioural test; there is no more reason to suppose that our beliefs / rules are any more valid than those of the person we are working with!

Note:

The ability to question rules and beliefs is one which the offenders needs to acquire *for themselves* if they are to be successful in the long term. This is another reason for us being collaborative - working *with* offenders to gradually develop their abilities at questioning rather than being adversarial and thereby causing them to become defensive of their own rules and beliefs.

CHAPTER 2.5

POSITIVE SELF-TALK

The concept of positive self-talk is a very appealing one to some therapists with a cognitive orientation, because of its constructive, optimistic and up-beat flavour. Whereas in the previous two chapters we have been talking about techniques which work at changing *maladaptive* thinking, in developing positive self-talk we look at the opposite side of the coin. Namely, developing clients' ability to think (or talk to themselves) in an *adaptive* fashion.

In some ways it is an extension of the methods we have talked about in the previous two chapters, because it hinges on producing alternative beliefs and alternative perceptions of situations, more positive than the clients' current beliefs and perceptions. It also makes use of the friend technique, the ability for clients to see their situation through the eyes of a good friend, someone who has their best interests at heart.

Indeed, it is this concept of "what would your own best friend" say, that is usually the most productive way of generating positive self-talk. So, if we consider our all-purpose example of the man who has his elbow jogged in the bar, and attacks the elbow-jogger, and then reports this incident to us in a subsequent session, we might say to him "What would your best friend have said to you, at the point when you had your elbow jogged and were feeling like attacking the guy who had jogged it?"

Many offenders are, unfortunately, adept at blocking such a question. For example, their replies might be

- *"I don't have a best friend"* or

- *"I don't know"* or

- *"He'd have told me to thump him I should think."*

This simply forces us back on some persistent ingenuity. For example we might say to the first response

- *"Yes, but if you did have a best friend what would he say?"*

and to the second,

- *"Well just have a think about it now, and try and imagine what he might have said - someone who has your own best interests at heart."*

And to the third,

- *"Yes but supposing your best friend really has your own best interest at heart, so doesn't want to see you get into trouble, end up in Court, and so forth, what would s/he say then?"*

This is a technique which can be used relentlessly, because of its positive nature. It doesn't have to be taken too heavily either, it often gives scope for some levity. It is basically a very upbeat way of looking at things.

It is usually a good idea for clients to practise talking to themselves "as though they are their own best friend." This does not have to be confined to situations where there is a risk of offending, it is a good idea to practise in all manner of situations, for example when one feels down, or worried. It is the skill of talking to oneself from the point of view of a helpful and encouraging outsider that we are trying to develop in clients.

The Be Your Own Best Friend form on the next page can be a very useful adjunct. The usual way of using it is to give clients three or four copies to last a week, and ask them to fill in as many as possible. Some people will do this, others won't, perhaps because they dislike forms. In either case, there is everything to be gained by going through the form with the client at the next session. If none have been filled in, it is best to fill the form in *with* the client, but commenting on it and analysing it as you go.

EXERCISE

Fill in the Be Your Own Best Friend form for yourself. To do this, you will probably have to think back to a moment in time when you were either tempted to do something you would have been better advised not to do. Once you have got a clear picture in your mind of the whole scene, then go ahead and complete the form.

BE YOUR OWN BEST FRIEND²

1. What are you feeling like doing? Rate how much you want to do it by giving it a number from 1 (slightly) to 100 (very much).

_____
_____
_____

2. What has triggered this off, if anything?

_____
_____
_____

3. What would a really good friend be saying to you, right now?

Remember, <u>a really good friend would certainly have your long-term best interests at heart</u>, and possibly ...

- Be reasoning with you. For example, telling you if you are:

    - over-emphasising one aspect of a situation and disregarding other, more positive aspects

    - thinking in an all or none fashion

    - jumping to conclusions

    - magnifying bad aspects and minimising good aspects of a situation

    - being over-influenced by one thing

    - 'mis-attributing' something - 'putting it down to' the wrong cause

- Be giving you good advice, for example:

    - *"Take yourself off home and wind down"*

    - *"Take no notice of what s/he says"*

    - *"Count to ten before you say anything"*

_____
_____
_____
_____
_____

EXERCISE

For this exercise, think of an offender you have worked with and fill the form in as you hope he would do. To do this you will have to bring to mind a particular moment in time in the offender's life, preferably when s/he was about to offend, or very tempted to offend. Then go ahead and complete the form as you hope he or she might have done.

BE YOUR OWN BEST FRIEND[2]

1. What are you feeling like doing? Rate how much you want to do it by giving it a number from 1 (slightly) to 100 (very much).

_____

_____

_____

2. What has triggered this off, if anything?

_____

_____

_____

3. What would a really good friend be saying to you, right now?

> Remember, <u>a really good friend would certainly have your long-term best interests at heart</u>, and possibly ...

- Be reasoning with you. For example, telling you if you are:

    - over-emphasising one aspect of a situation and disregarding other, more positive aspects

    - thinking in an all or none fashion

    - jumping to conclusions

    - magnifying bad aspects and minimising good aspects of a situation

    - being over-influenced by one thing

    - 'mis-attributing' something - 'putting it down to' the wrong cause

- Be giving you good advice, for example:

    - "Take yourself off home and wind down"

    - "Take no notice of what s/he says"

    - "Count to ten before you say anything"

_____

_____

_____

_____

_____

 **DISCUSSION**

Hopefully you found these two exercises reasonably straightforward, although perhaps the second was somewhat more difficult than the first. The main difficulty, sometimes, is thinking of a particular moment in time when the completion of this form would be relevant, either for you (in the first exercise) or your client (in the second exercise).

The purpose of completing the forms is really only a stepping stone to developing the skill of talking positively to oneself at will. Many people take very readily to this concept, others need some more work. In either case there are various stages along the way, the following being the main ones:

1. The client can "see what we mean" when we give examples of positive self-talk in the kind of situations that are relevant to them.

2. The client can produce some examples of relevant positive self-talk, for *us* to write down on the Be Your Own Best Friend form.

3. The client can write down examples of positive self-talk, *under our supervision.*

4. The client can write down relevant examples of positive self-talk, *independently.*

5. The client can produce positive self-talk, when talking out loud.

6. Finally, the client can produce positive self-talk, sub-vocally.

This makes it sound rather a laborious process, which it usually is not. Usually, some of these stages are skipped, and sometimes clients can leap straight to the final stage, or the penultimate one, once they have had the concept explained to them. In any event, it is an extremely powerful cognitive method which is well worth the time it takes to master it thoroughly.

CHAPTER 2.6

RELAXATION

A relaxation method can be legitimately included in a programme on cognitive approaches because the technique described here can in some ways be thought of as a cognitive relaxation technique. Frankly, even if it couldn't be included legitimately, we would still have to put it in simply because a good method of reducing physiological arousal level is so important when working with offenders.

It is clear that our cognitive functioning is grossly affected by big swings in physiological arousal level. So, someone who is extremely agitated can perceive events quite differently from when he or she is in a calm state: a comment that would be interpreted as "a leg-pull" when one is calm, can be interpreted as a challenging insult when agitated. The results of seeing it this way can of course be very serious.

So the purpose of a good relaxation method is (a) to keep an individual's physiological arousal level within reasonable limits day in day out, so that, when something agitating occurs, the arousal level does not shoot into dangerously high levels, and (b) to give individuals a means of coping when they feel their agitation rising; an immediate measure they can take to reduce that level.

There are many good and effective forms of relaxation and training. Three categories are:

- techniques involving muscle relaxation

- techniques involving fantasy and

- "cognitive" techniques

The technique described in this chapter falls under the third heading and is based on Benson's technique. What Benson did was, broadly speaking, to re-phrase some ideas which are currently Yoga techniques into language which is more acceptable in the Western World. So this method revolves around calm, natural breathing, saying a soothing word to oneself (otherwise known as a mantra), and developing a passive attitude.

What follows is the verbatim account of the instructions I use for teaching relaxation.

A COGNITIVE RELAXATION METHOD: VERBATIM SCRIPT

"So now we are going to learn how to relax. And this is perfectly easy. The first thing we have to do is simply to sit comfortably in a chair. It can be done lying down or wherever you like, but a chair is as good as anywhere.

When you are comfortable, simply close your eyes and then take one deep breath in ... and then exhale smoothly out. Good. And that's the last deep breath that we take. From now on we simply breathe ordinarily. Just smooth, ordinary, breathing.

What I want you to do is to concentrate on doing just that for a minute or so. I'll keep quiet during that time, you just concentrate on breathing ordinarily. Ordinary breathing. Not shallow breathing, not deep breathing, just ordinary breathing.

(A minute's silence.)

That's good. Now the next step is simply to say "smooth" to yourself as you breathe out. Not out loud, just quietly to yourself. On each out-breath, just say "smooth."

Just practise that for another minute or so. Say in a reassuring sort of tone to yourself "smooth," every time you breathe out.

(Another minute's silence.)

That's very good. Now there's only one more component, and that is to feel a passive attitude. And that's easier than it sounds. All we do is say to ourselves that for 5 minutes nothing matters. Just for 5 minutes, nothing matters. So that thoughts can come into our heads and go out of our heads again - let thoughts come in and thoughts go out - it doesn't matter what we think. Noises can go on inside the room or outside the room, and they don't matter. It doesn't matter what happens, just for 5 minutes. It doesn't matter what's happening around us or what we are thinking, what noises are happening. Nothing matters, just for 5 minutes.

So see if you can feel that lovely passive attitude, that nothing matters just for 5 minutes. Feel that lovely passive attitude. Keep the breathing nice and smooth, nice and easy, and just for 5 minutes enjoy some relaxation.

I'm going to keep quiet during that 5 minutes, and when we get towards the end of that time I'll count from 3 backwards to 1 and that will tell us that the 5 minutes is nearly up. So just relax for 5 minutes and I'll tell you when the time is up.

(5 minute's silence.)

Five minutes is nearly up, so in a moment I'll start to count backwards from 3 to 1. When I get to 1 I'd like you to start opening your eyes, have a stretch if you want to, and come slowly back to the room you are in.

3 ... 2 ... 1.

So now open your eyes gradually, have a stretch if you want to, and slowly come back to life. Good.

Now you're back into an ordinary state, the thing to remember is that 5 minutes relaxation per day is splendid. Come what may, have a 5 minute slot every day for relaxing and playing the tape. Just sit down and relax. Have a regular time every day, where you do that without fail.

Equally, it is good for us to be as relaxed as possible all the time. So it's always a good thing to be as relaxed as we can be whatever we are doing. So try and get a little bit of relaxation - a little bit of that passive attitude - into everyday life, as well as just for the 5 minute slot. Be as relaxed as possible in the rest of life as well.

That's all there is on this tape, so if you rewind it now it will be ready for playing tomorrow."

EXERCISE

Find a partner to practise on if you can, or, failing that, practice talking to an empty chair. Either way, read aloud the relaxation instructions you have just read, in real time. In other words, leave the appropriate spaces when you are meant to be quiet. Also, follow your own instructions, in other words breathe as you say you should, say "smooth" as you are meant to, and work on developing a passive attitude. If you have a cassette tape machine, produce a cassette of the relaxation text. Then replay the tape, following the instructions yourself.

The advantages of this relaxation method are several, but specifically:

It is a method that is easily generalisable; you don't have to be lying down or in any special circumstances. It can be done anywhere.

At least two of the three instructions can be carried out even when other activities are taking place too. Breathing can always be reasonably calm and natural, and we can say a soothing word to ourselves if we wish. To some extent, we can also develop, at least partially, a passive attitude under most circumstances. Clients should be instructed to use the relaxation method in two ways:

1. **At least once daily to generate a reasonably low level of overall physiological arousal and,**

2. **Whenever they feel themselves being made tense by events. To interpret that tension as a cue for deliberately relaxing.**

So, for clients who need a relaxation method, notably people with temper control problems, it is quite a significant undertaking, we have to encourage their commitment to it. Fortunately, however, this method is a reasonably enjoyable one as well as being effective. The commitment, therefore, need not be an onerous one.

CHAPTER 2.7

SCHEDULING

Scheduling is a good strong pro-active technique. It is often considered to be a behavioural one because it looks at what one is going to *do* over a period of time, usually the next week. In other words one plans the forthcoming week, or, at least, some key activities over that time. It is especially relevant in two ways

- When we can see that there are particularly at-risk times in terms of the client's offending. In that case it may be possible to schedule clear alternative activities.

  - For example, one sex-offender, who knew that he was under particular risk at the lunch break and end of day of the local junior school, scheduled a regular pattern of activities which kept him busy and away from the vicinity of the school at those times. Although this was only one element in his treatment, it was a significant one.

- To stress to an offender that it is perfectly possible to take charge of one's life, to plan out what is going to happen and to ensure that it does. Thereby to empower offenders to take proper control over their lives.

Its use is very simple. We normally use the form overleaf, or one similar to it, and plan out with the client what he or she will do over the next week, or whatever period of time it is until we next meet. Three 'tips':

  - It is easy to become over-optimistic, and plan a schedule of activities which reads well but stands little chance of really happening. Clients are sometimes as susceptible to this temptation as we ourselves are, so it is our job to ensure that what emerges is realistic and achievable.

  - With some clients it is clear that the gap from planning the schedule with them to the next meeting is too long and there is nothing we can do about it. It can be useful in those circumstances to have the client 'phone us to let us know that specific targets have been achieved. Although this might appear to be an over-onerous task which the client would resist, some clients seem actively to appreciate this idea as proof that somebody cares.

  - Usually, when we next meet, and compare what actually happened with what we scheduled, the two do not match up perfectly; the client has 'failed' in one or two aspects. It is generally helpful to have a degree of flexibility here if we are to maintain the client's perception that they are beginning to get a firm grasp on life.

Weekly Activity Schedule

	M	T	W	T	F	S	S
9-10							
10-11							
11-12							
12-1							
1-2							
2-3							
3-4							
4-5							
5-6							
6-7							
7-8							
8-12							

CHAPTER 2.8

RECORD-KEEPING

Record-Keeping is exactly as it says. The client simply keeps a record of what they have done, day by day, and thereby produces a record for the *past* week. This has a variety of purposes, specifically:

- To demonstrate to clients who say (for example) 'I can never control my temper' that this is not *always* so. There will be times when the client resists offending in spite of 'provocation', *and these are the very instances to consider in therapy.*

- To obtain a record of current offending.

- To enable the therapist to get a clearer picture of exactly what is happening out of therapy, and thereby

- For both therapist and client to have a record of progress.

Record-keeping can be used by itself, and may frequently be the first measure that a therapist takes, simply in order to 'get a handle on' the person's offending. Even so, there is often a significant pay-off in that the mere act of recording activities sometimes reduces the frequency of actions we are trying to reduce or eliminate.

(Plainly, if we have **scheduled** a client's activities with him or her, we will need to have a record of what actually happens, otherwise neither of us will know just how useful the scheduling was or what direction we now need to head in. However, such a record can be kept simply by the client ticking off what they actually achieve, on the scheduling sheet, rather than have a separate record-keeping sheet. With clients as with most of us, there is some advantage in keeping paperwork to a minimum.)

Overall, *record-keeping* can give the client a more accurate perspective on current events, *scheduling* can give a client a greater feeling of control when they feel buffeted by circumstances and events. Both therapist and client may feel that both techniques give them a better grasp of what is happening.

Weekly Record Form

	M	T	W	T	F	S	S
9-10							
10-11							
11-12							
12-1							
1-2							
2-3							
3-4							
4-5							
5-6							
6-7							
7-8							
8-12							

EXERCISE

This is a major exercise, and an important one, because it gives us an insight into what we are asking of our clients.

Part One: Take a copy of the scheduling form on page 66 and schedule your forthcoming week, taking care to pay heed to the guidelines given. Take plenty of time; you are, after all, planning out a week of your life.

Part Two: Tick those items you achieve, as each day goes past over the next week. This, clearly, gives a record of what you have done. Note the reasons for any discrepancies between what you planned and what you achieve.

CHAPTER 2.9

DISTRACTION

Some examples of distraction are as follows:

- An agoraphobic person, feeling agitated riding on a bus, might distract themselves by concentrating on all the people and shops that pass, the other side of the window.

- A patient at the dentist, with a vivid fear of dentists, may distract themselves by concentrating on exactly what the dentist is doing. Usually, any pain experienced is nowhere near that which is fantasized about by the fearful patient.

- A man who has his elbow jogged in the bar, may distract himself by concentrating on exactly what the elbow jogger does immediately after. This will distract him from his own inner feelings of intense rage.

- A sex offender sitting on a sofa watching TV alone with his 12 year old niece, may distract himself by concentrating on the TV.

- Shoplifters, in a bookshop, may distract themselves by concentrating on the books themselves, rather than thoughts of stealing them.

One observation you might have, reading the above examples, is that each one depends upon the person being *motivated* to distract themselves. For example our jogged-elbow man needs to be motivated not to get into a fight and therefore be prepared to implement this distraction technique. Our sex offender needs to be motivated to resist re-offending. Our shop lifter is motivated similarly.

A second observation is that the distraction needs to have been rehearsed in advance. In the heat of the moment there is little chance of the individual thinking out this strategy for themselves. It needs to have been talked through and thoroughly rehearsed with yourself.

These two observations notwithstanding, distraction is a very simple technique and is sometimes quite astonishingly effective. One of the reasons for this may be that it "empowers" would-be offenders; it immediately gives them something that they can do and which feels effective.

> **Note:** Some people advocate "prepared distraction tasks" such as "think of an animal beginning with A, then an animal beginning with B, than an animal beginning with C, and so on. In my experience this approach is not nearly so effective as the "distraction to reality" approach exampled above.

COGNITIVE SELF-TEST, MODULE 2.

Again, there is no need to write anything, just read the questions and compose mental answers. Check back to the text if you wish, but do not move on until you are happy that you can securely answer all the questions without referring back.

1
Name four ways of *identifying* a person's automatic thoughts.

2
One way that you might have mentioned in question one is the use of diary forms. Name one specific problem with this purely verbal method.

3
A major way of *changing* maladaptive automatic thinking is by using Socratic dialogue. How would you define Socratic dialogue?

4
On page 42, we discussed how to think of the kind of questions that go to make up a Socratic dialogue. One way was simply to take our time and mull things over between sessions. But we also used an acronym to remind us of four other specific types of question. What is the acronym, and what do the letters stand for?

5
One problem that can occur when asking Socratic-type questions is that we can come across as 'smart'. How can we guard against this?

6
We said that we generally identify people's *beliefs and rules* in much the same way as we identify their automatic thinking. However, there is one additional technique we can use. What is it?

7
In changing people's beliefs and rules we again use similar methods to when we change their automatic thinking. However, there are two additional methods. What are they?

8
On page 53 we mention that all the techniques we discuss hinge on one thing. What is it?

9
On page 54 we talk about positive self-talk, and say that it could be considered as different from the methods we have so far discussed (which look at changing maladaptive thinking and beliefs). In what way could it be considered as different?

10
Imagine you are motoring through a busy street in town, late for an appointment, when someone 'cuts you up', cuts straight in front of you, causing you to brake sharply and taking your place in the queue. Shortly after, you both have to stop at a red light, and you are about to get out of the car to remonstrate with the other driver. What might an ideal 'best friend' say to you?

11
What are the three components of Benson's relaxation method?

12
Why, in your opinion, is relaxation such an effective technique with people with anger management problems?

13
Although Scheduling and Record-Keeping use virtually the same form they are different. In what way?

14
Scheduling and Record-Keeping are often considered to be Behavioural techniques. Yet the fact that they can alter people's thinking about themselves (and their lives) also entitles them to be considered as cognitive techniques. In what way can they alter one's thinking about oneself and one's life?

15
Why do you think that 'distraction with reality' (the sort we give examples of on page 69) might be more realistic and helpful than 'prepared distraction tasks' like 'think of an animal beginning with A, etc'?

MODULE THREE:

MAKING IT WORK

AIMS

To learn how to apply the principles and techniques described in modules one and two. Specifically:

- To examine the therapist-skills and therapist-qualities that are necessary.

- To examine the importance of a collaborative relationship between helper and helped.

- To examine the structure of initial, intermediate and concluding treatment sessions.

- To examine group approaches to treatment.

CHAPTER 3.1

THE SKILLS AND QUALITIES NECESSARY TO APPLY A COGNITIVE APPROACH

INTRODUCTION

There is no doubt that the personal characteristics of the helper or therapist are astonishingly relevant. In a study cited by Lambert (1989), Crits-Christoph et al looked at the effect of psychological treatments in four big centres in the United States, examined the variance in treatment results and found that the therapist accounted for eight times more variance than the treatment technique used. To simplify only a little, it is eight times more important who treats an individual than what technique is employed. Any idea, therefore, that a cognitive approach is some kind of panacea which can be employed by anyone who takes the trouble to learn the technique is clearly a myth.

A graphic example of how therapists can effect their clients was published by Ricks in 1974 who looked at what had become of a group of adolescent boys who had been treated some years previously when they were experiencing very high degrees of anxiety, vulnerability, feelings of unreality and isolation. The boys had been seen by one of two therapists in a child guidance clinic. The long term outcome produced by these two therapists was no different for less disturbed boys, but there was a very large difference in the outcomes with the more disturbed boys.

One therapist, whom Ricks labelled "supershrink" produced an outcome whereby only 27% of his cases became schizophrenic in adulthood. Those cases seen by therapist B, later labelled "pseudoshrink", however, yielded an 84% rate of schizophrenia in adulthood. (Bear in mind, when thinking of these as very high rates, that Ricks was only looking at what happened to the more disturbed individuals.) Although the clients were not randomly assigned between therapists A and B, the caseloads were similar.

Ricks looked at the differences in styles between therapist A and therapist B. It transpired that therapist A devoted far more time to those who were disturbed, while the less successful therapist, B, did the opposite. Therapist A, supershrink, tended to be firm and direct with parents, supported the youngsters' increasing independence, and helped them develop problem-solving capabilities for everyday life. All against the background of a strong therapeutic relationship.

Therapist B, pseudoshrink, on the other hand moved rapidly into "deep material" and Ricks speculates that he may have increased the youngsters' feelings of anxiety, vulnerability, unreality and alienation, without being able to help the boys develop ways of coping with those feelings.

Similarly Luborsky et al (1985) describe their analysis of the outcome of clients seen by nine different therapists. Importantly, treatment manuals were used to guide the delivery of the comparison treatments. In other words, not only were therapists trained to deliver the prescribed treatment, but their work was supervised and monitored to check they were doing what was intended. One might reasonably assume that individual differences between therapists were therefore minimised. Even so, in spite of this careful selection, training, monitoring and supervision, therapists displayed highly divergent results. The patients of therapist A, for example (a different individual from supershrink) showed substantial improvement on a wide variety of outcomes, while C's patients averaged little improvement and on some criteria actually showed an average *negative* change.

Again, Orlinsky and Howard (1980) described the outcome of 143 female cases seen by 23 therapists offering a range of traditional verbal psychotherapy. Of the 23 therapists, 6 were + rated which meant that 70% of their cases were improved and no more than 10% deteriorated, or at least 40% were "considerably improved" and no cases worse. On the other hand, 5 of these 23 therapists were X-rated, which means that 50% or less of the cases were rated as improved while more than 10% were rated as worse. Orlinsky and Howard demonstrated that professional degree and age were not strongly correlated to outcome. However, over six years experience was associated with better outcomes.

In summary, we would be foolhardy to suppose that even a technique such as a cognitive approach, which is widely regarded as a "strong" technique, can overcome the vicissitudes of the individual delivering it. We therefore need to pay a good deal of attention to the individual characteristics of us therapists.

EXERCISE

This is an important but sensitive exercise; please read right to the end of this page before starting it.

Clearly the personal characteristics of the helper/therapist are very important. Also, what we have discussed about cognitive approaches in the previous two modules suggests that certain specific skills may be required. Please think of a colleague of yours who you know has a high degree of success with their clients and describe his or her characteristics here:

Characteristics of colleague who has a high rate of success:

_____
_____
_____
_____
_____
_____

Now think of a colleague who does not have a high degree of success, and fill in their characteristics here:

Characteristic of colleague who does not have a high rate of success:

_____
_____
_____
_____
_____
_____
_____
_____

Notes:
In completing this exercise I suggest you ensure that nothing you write would identify the individuals you have in mind.
Try not to be too 'philosophical' about the meaning of the word 'successful'; take it to mean the stopping of offenders offending!

TURN TO NEXT PAGE FOR DISCUSSION

Discussion of Exercise:

Some of the skills and qualities necessary to pursue a cognitive approach follow logically from what we have said about its nature, both in terms of its content and the manner of carrying it out. Below I divide them into (a) skills and (b) qualities, which is only partly satisfactory because the two overlap.

Nevertheless:

SKILLS:

1. **An understanding of the *Cognitive model*** as it applies to offenders. That is, to understand how early experience results in particular beliefs and particular ways of looking at oneself and others, and how those beliefs and views result in present-day thinking, or 'automatic thoughts', and behaviour.

2. **The ability and inclination to conduct a behavioural analysis** ...

   - *"When do you get these thoughts?"* ...

   - *"What was going on before you started thinking this?"* ...

   - *"What happened afterwards?"*.

   - Do the thoughts seem to be serving some kind of function that has not been recognised?

3. **The ability *to negotiate the objectives of treatment*** and proceed with treatment along the lines of what has been established. This facilitates the maintenance of the person's motivation to change.

4. **To monitor progress** and evaluate what is happening.

5. **To teach ways of generalising progress**, for example by teaching coping-strategies for incidents which would normally produce anger.

QUALITIES:

1. *Collaboration:* **the ability to form a collaborative alliance** with the client, rather than adopting the 'expert' role. As we have said earlier, this can be demanding on the helper, and might imply that he or she will need to be adept at sometimes obtaining support from colleagues or friends.

2. *Gentleness.* This is regarded as important because questioning is one of the important tools of a Cognitive Approach. This can seem harsh unless the therapist exhibits a degree of gentleness. You may remember the following hypothetical conversation from Module Two, which unearthed a belief / rule:

Us: How did the offence come about?
Client: There wasn't really an offence
Us: So what happened in the incident that led to you being convicted?
Client: We went back to her flat, and things went on from there.
Us: Things went on from there?
Client: We went to bed.
Us: Was she agreeable to that?
Client: Yes, I think so.
Us: What made you think that?
Client: I just thought she was.
Us: What made you think that?
Client: She didn't put up much of a fight.
Us: But she put up some sort of fight?
Client: Yes, but *when women say No they don't really mean it.*

It is all too easy to see how such an interchange could be very confrontational if done without gentleness. If so, it is most likely to be counterproductive.

> **Does our compassion for the victim mean we can have none for the offender?**

3. *The ability to listen.* Important because the therapist has to pick up not only the explicit content of what is said but also the characteristic thinking styles (eg all or none thinking) and beliefs (eg It is dangerous to trust other people).

4. *A professional manner,* adhering to the structure of the sessions, tackling the agenda of the sessions in a systematic way and being responsible for effectively using the time available. This is regarded as particularly important in the cognitive approach because there are generally specific goals to be achieved, in a limited number of sessions, each of a specified duration.

5. *Ingenuity*. Sometimes the therapist will have to improvise techniques to tackle specific problems and thinking styles. Imagination and initiative in this regard are relevant too.

6. *A lightness of touch*. Although humour can be badly judged, its judicious use can alter a person's perspective on a situation and create a bond between therapist and client. So in this context 'humour' will probably take the form of lack of solemnity, rather than cracking jokes.

7. *The ability to help the client to develop a commitment to change*. Clients' motivation to change has long been held as a key element in successful outcome, but in forensic work the therapist frequently has to assume some responsibility for developing this.

CHAPTER 3.2

THE THERAPIST-CLIENT RELATIONSHIP

It is probably worth spending a little more time thinking about the relationship between the helper and the helped, because of the powerful findings of Lambert and Goleman, both referred to earlier. Also because, with offenders, the relationship can be a difficult area for the helper to get right. Although Probation Officers, for example, have long had the idea of 'getting alongside' the offender, some Probation Officers feel that this has become out of fashion, perhaps because it can feel as though one is actually colluding with the client. This is a pity, if one wants to adopt a cognitive approach, because 'getting alongside' is very similar to the cognitive approach's 'Collaborative' nature.

EXERCISE

Please place in order of importance the following elements, all of which are relevant to forming a relationship between helper and helped. Place a '1' by the one you judge to be most important, a '2' by the second most important, and so on. Note any reasons you have for giving particular importance to some items and less to others.

- Genuineness

- Asking 'open' questions

- Liking the client

- Empathy

- Understanding the client's problems and 'where they're coming from'

- The ability to summarise accurately what has gone on so far in the treatment session

- Warmth

- The ability to reflect the content and emotion of what the client says

- Unconditional positive regard.

Then go on and read the summary ("The Therapist-Client Relationship) on the next page.

Discussion of Exercise:

THE THERAPIST-CLIENT RELATIONSHIP

The highest level of relationship is where the therapist both values and understands the client, and the client is aware of that.

- Valuing

- Understanding

The middle level is where the therapist conveys the qualities associated with effective therapists, and which are likely to result in the client feeling that s/he is valued and understood:

- Empathy

- Warmth

- Genuineness

- Unconditional positive regard

The lowest level is expertise in *skills* traditionally associated with effective therapists

- asking 'open' questions

- reflecting the content and emotion of what the client says

- summarising

- commenting accurately on the 'process', etc

The higher levels are more important than the lower ones. So, if the therapist manages to convey the middle level qualities (empathy, warmth, genuineness) it is of less importance whether s/he is adept in the lower level skills ('open' questions, reflections, etc.) Similarly, if the therapist manages to convey that the client is understood and valued (the highest level) it matters less how much empathy warmth and genuineness have been evident (although clearly they probably will have been). Nevertheless, it is sometimes essential to have mastery of lower order skills to achieve the higher order outcomes.

Note: This page has no pictures, no boxes, looks rather boring. Nevertheless, I would suggest to you that this is one of the most important pages in the entire book.

But why, in the cognitive approach are these personal qualities, skills, and the relationship between us and the offender so important? We can see, examining each skill, or each personal characteristic, why that particular one is important, but there is also a more global reason.

Ultimately we are trying to change the offender's *views* of himself or herself, and also their views of others and the world around them. (See Module 1, page 6, para 2.) These views form the deepest level of the three levels we examine, deeper than the person's beliefs or their automatic thoughts.

Supposing, then, that an offender holds a view of others as predominantly antagonistic, hostile, difficult and untrustworthy, how can could we disabuse him of these views? Talking and persuading might be one method, but a much more direct and striking method is for therapists themselves to demonstrate qualities quite different from those and to forge a relationship which contradicts the offender's previous view of how others are.

Contrast this with how some professionals believe that they must "come on strong" with offenders, and leave them in no doubt of the wrongness of what they have done. Whilst it might be possible to argue a case for this from some sort of justice or revenge model, it is difficult to square with a cognitive approach because such 'coming on strong' simply reaffirms the offender's belief that other people are hostile and un-accepting, and that he is somehow different and alienated.

Similarly, if an offender has a view of himself as inadequate, one of the most powerful ways of disabusing him of this view is for him to see himself in an equal, collaborative relationship with someone who appears to be "professional and effective". In practice, the offender is then experiencing being an effective, competent person. Clearly this is likely to be a much more powerful approach than simple verbal persuasion where an "expert" strongly tells an offender that he is really more competent than he believes, but the very nature of the interaction demonstrates the offender's lowly position.

In summary, although consideration of therapist characteristics and the relationship in therapy can at first sight appear to be peripheral, in fact exactly the reverse is the case. It may be just these factors, the therapist characteristics and the relationship which is formed, that reach right to the heart of the cognitive approach. Beyond negative automatic thoughts, through dysfunctional beliefs and into the views that the person holds of himself and of others.

EXERCISE

Below is a list of the skills and qualities we have discussed. Go through the whole list rating yourself on each one by placing a number from 1 (bad) to 10 (good) alongside each. This is an exercise you might like to come back from time to time so a copiable sheet is enclosed at the end.

❖ Understands the Cognitive model.

❖ Has the ability and inclination to conduct a behavioural analysis, asking 'when does it happen', 'what triggers it', what are the consequences' etc.

❖ Has the ability to negotiate the objectives of treatment

❖ Monitors progress and evaluates what is happening.

❖ Teaches ways of generalising progress, for example by teaching coping-strategies for incidents which would normally produce anger.

❖ Is empathic.

❖ Is energetic and optimistic.

❖ Is persistent ... does not give up easily.

❖ Has the ability to form a collaborative alliance with the client.

❖ Is gentle, does not lecture or harangue but relies more on guided discovery.

❖ Has the ability to listen.

❖ Has a professional manner, adhering to the structure of the sessions, tackling the agenda of the sessions in a systematic way and being responsible for effectively using the time available.

❖ Has ingenuity, thinking of good ideas for tackling problems.

❖ Has a lightness of touch, is not too solemn.

❖ Has the ability to help the client to develop a commitment to change.

❖ Is genuine.

❖ Accepts and values clients.

❖ Understands the client's problems and 'where they're coming from'.

❖ Has an appropriate degree of warmth, is neither remote nor 'over-does it'.

CHAPTER 3.3

THE PRINCIPLES IN PRACTICE: WORKING WITH INDIVIDUALS

Introduction:

This chapter is somewhat different from the preceding ones in that there are few exercises to complete. The sub-chapters describe an effective way to lay out your sessions if you are working with an individual and employing a cognitive approach. Effectively, then, these sub-chapters form 'check-lists' of what you should be doing in each of the sessions.

The sub-chapters are titled as follows:

3.3A THE ASSESSMENT INTERVIEW

3.3B BETWEEN THE ASSESSMENT INTERVIEW AND THE SECOND INTERVIEW

3.3C THE SECOND INTERVIEW

3.3D TREATMENT SESSIONS

3.3E ENDING THERAPY

3.3A

THE ASSESSMENT INTERVIEW

The aim of the first interview is to

- discover the nature and extent of the client's offending

- to obtain sufficient information to decide upon an effective intervention.

Some authors suggest that a full assessment interview is not necessary in a Cognitive approach. That may or may not be so, but there seems little to be lost be completing a full interview, especially as, at this stage you cannot be sure you will be adopting a Cognitive approach.

In other words you will probably aim to cover the following:
- Offending behaviour:
    - nature, (what is done, how does it come about, *including any automatic thoughts at the time, or insight into the offender's belief system* given by his description of the offence).

    - duration (how long has it been going on for)

    - frequency (how often does it happen)

    - severity (how serious is it).

- Previous and current interventions/treatment. Any current medication.

- Domestic situation and history, including childhood.

- Employment situation and history, including schooling.

- Social contacts.

- Previous traumas, and any previous psychological disturbance.

- Physical: amount of exercise taken, appetite, sleep pattern.

- Any notable medical aspects.

- Consumption of alcohol, non-prescribed drugs, tobacco, caffeine (via: coffee, including instant; tea [equivalent to instant coffee]; Cola drinks).

- Client's view of causes of offending, and their thoughts, if any, on how to stop.

- Client's own goals.

On the next page you will find a form which you may use for the initial interview.

Date of Assessment _____ *Client Name* _____

Check-list:

- Offending behaviour. Duration, frequency, severity.

- Previous and current treatment. Current medication if any.

- Domestic situation and history.

- Employment situation and history.

- Social contacts.

- Previous traumas, and any previous psychological disturbance

- Physical: exercise, appetite, sleep pattern.

- Any notable medical aspects.

- Consumption of alcohol, non-prescribed drugs, tobacco, caffeine.

- Client's view of causes of offending, and any plan for its resolution.

- Client's own goals.

*Notes*_____

_____

_____

_____

_____

_____

_____

_____

_____

_____

_____

_____

_____

_____

_____

Notes on the assessment interview:

1. Clearly the first thing to do in the assessment interview is to explain to the offender that it is just that. *Exactly* what you say will depend on the context in which you work, but the main points to convey are that

   - it is their chance to tell you all about themselves, including their offending

   - it is your chance to ask them about themselves, and

   - the two of you will hopefully be working together to address their offending.

   Exactly how you do this will no doubt depend on your own inimitable style.

2. Although the listing of the topics to be covered makes it appear somewhat like an interrogation, that is not the intention. The skill is in being able to *cover all the ground in a systematic but gentle way,* allowing a variation in the order of topics if that seems sensible. For example, *many offenders might be sensitive about their offending being the first point of discussion* so it may be advisable in such cases to start with a less contentious topic, such as their upbringing and childhood. This is not solely for reasons of gentleness, it may result in more information being obtained.

3. *Do take notes during the first interview*, there is no way you will be able to remember all the data you will gather until after the person has left. Quite reasonable, many therapists believe that note-taking inhibits the natural flow between them and the client, and for this reason we do not normally take notes after the first session. This first session is, however, the assessment interview, and for that we need to take notes.

4. At the end of the first interview you should have a great deal of information to assimilate. **It is usually a mistake to give your 'first impressions' to the person at the end of the interview,** because the assimilation of the information gathered takes time and thought. Much better to say something like *"Well, we need to look towards drawing to a close shortly ... what I want to do is to think about all you have said and have a think what might be the best way of us tackling things, then next time we meet we can put together a plan of action ... okay? Before we go though, is there anything else you think you should tell me ... or anything you want to ask me?"* And proceed to make another appointment.

3.3B

BETWEEN THE ASSESSMENT INTERVIEW AND THE SECOND INTERVIEW

In between the first and second interviews we have to decide on our plan of action - what our treatment strategy will be - and to write it down. To do this we have to absolutely clear on three things:

- What the offender's problems are. That is, primarily, what offences are committed.

- What our treatment goals are. Hopefully we will be able to agree these with the offender, but this is not always the case.

- Our plans for achieving these goals.

This phase, between first and second interview, is probably the single most important section of treatment, because it largely determines what we will do for the remainder of our contact with the individual concerned.

There are several points to bear in mind:

➤ In relation to describing the offender's presenting problem

- Stick to overt, observable phenomena. For example 'Gets into fights' or 'Steals cars' or 'Assaults women'. We can be reluctant to do this because it doesn't sound clever enough. However, if we immediately evoke some covert underlying mechanisms such as, respectively, 'Has macho self-image' or 'Has low self-esteem' or 'Has poor social skills' we may be directing our therapeutic effort down the wrong lines.

- It may be that there are several problems, all clearly connected with offending. If this is so, we should of course write them down. If on the other hand the person offends and also has lots of other, unconnected, problems, just as any one of us taken from the street might have a range of problems at any particular time, it is not fruitful to record those.

➤ In relation to describing the treatment goals

- Again, stick to clear, observable and measurable phenomena, usually the opposite side of the coin from the problems above. For example 'Not to get into fights', 'Not to steal cars', 'Not to assault women', rather than 'To come to terms with his aggression', 'To come to terms with inner envy and need for excitement' or 'To examine issues relating to gender'.

- You might ask why we should wish to write down such apparently banal goals, and the answer is: simply to keep us on track when we come to write the third section which is ...

➢ The treatment plan, the main points about which are

- There should be a clear, direct, logical link between the elements of the treatment plan and the treatment goals. When we describe to an imaginary outside person what we are planning to do and they say 'Why' we must have an indisputable answer.

- For example if we are treating someone whose problem is getting into fights, the goal for whom is not to get into fights, we might have a treatment plan of (a) teaching relaxation; (b) teaching the person not to jump to (negative) conclusions; and (c) generating a more positive view of other people in our client. If asked 'Why' the answers might be: (a) 'He is very agitated, some times more than others, and the more agitated he is the more likely he is to misinterpret things, take them wrongly and get into a fight ... we have shown that from his record keeping. So, if we can reduce his level of agitation that will be a pressure in the right direction.' (b) 'The most frequent cause of fights for this particular person is jumping to the conclusion that someone is trying to show him up. Therefore, if we can prevent that happening, there should be less chance of a fight developing.' (c) 'It seems as though his negative view of other people leads him to be very suspicious of them, always suspecting that they might be about to try to make a fool of him. If we could convince him that although this might have been true at one stage in his life, it no longer is now, or only rarely at any rate, we would undermine the *cause* of jumping to conclusions.'

If on the other hand we said we were going to (a) boost the person's self esteem, (b) encourage less macho interests, and (c) help with budgeting, which is causing great difficulties, we may not be able to make a direct link with offending, even though the interventions themselves may be very laudable ones and entirely appropriate for another client.

EXERCISE:

On the next two pages you will find two Overview forms. Fill them in for two clients you are currently working with, and then check back to the guide-lines you have just read and see how what you have written matches up.

NOTES:

_____

_____

_____

_____

_____

_____

_____

_____

_____

_____

_____

_____

_____

_____

_____

_____

_____

OVERVIEW *to be completed after the first interview*

Client: Name_____DoB_____

Offending behaviour:

_____
_____
_____
_____
_____
_____
_____

The Overall Goal(s) of Intervention. This will normally be agreed with the client:

_____
_____
_____
_____
_____
_____
_____

The Overall Plan for achieving the above goals:

_____
_____
_____
_____
_____
_____
_____

Any Other Comments:

_____

OVERVIEW *to be completed after the first interview*

Client: Name_____DoB_____

Offending behaviour:

_____
_____
_____
_____
_____
_____

The Overall Goal(s) of Intervention. This will normally be agreed with the client:

_____
_____
_____
_____
_____
_____
_____

The Overall Plan for achieving the above goals:

_____
_____
_____
_____
_____
_____
_____

Any Other Comments:

_____

3.3C
THE SECOND INTERVIEW

In the second interview, having had a little time to dwell over the initial interview, you will aim to:

- **Agree a conceptualisation of the client's offending.** To agree 'what is going on'. **If possible, to form agreed goals.**

It does sometimes happen, in forensic work, that the goals cannot be agreed between ourselves and the client.

One prisoner I saw was insistent that he would shoot six prison-officers he alleged had beaten him up, on release from prison. This was plainly worrying, especially as he was already in prison for having shot another person. Most professionals would probably agree that they would wish to work against such goals. After all, most people intervening with offenders are, effectively, employed by society to encourage clients to comply with its expectations. He, however, was perfectly happy with his intentions, and more than resigned, thereafter, to spend the rest of his days in prison, secure in the knowledge that at least he would become notorious. Although this case had an eventual happy ending, it was clearly impossible to come to an agreement on the goal of treatment. Indeed, any attempt to do so risked losing him from contact altogether.

If it is not possible to agree, you should at least have clear goals in your own mind. (And written down on the Overview sheet.) This is less satisfactory than having agreed goals, and in this case it is probably best to keep your goals to yourself. However, it is sometimes perfectly acceptable to say something along the lines of: *"The situation seems to be that you are content to carry on offending, but I will be trying to persuade you that you would be better off not doing."* So long as the 'lightness of touch' is maintained, the 'straightness' of this can be effective.

- **Explain the cognitive approach, and gain the client's commitment to it.** How you describe the cognitive approach is up to you, but it might be something along the lines of: *"We will be working on this jointly, discussing things together and deciding what to do. We will try to work systematically, and there will probably be things to do in between our sessions. In particular, we will be looking at how you think, the kind of rules you have for the way the world should operate, and generally how you view yourself and other people. But importantly, we will look at how all those things effect what you do and the way you feel about it."* For some people such a description is informative and useful. For others, a much abbreviated version is better, even just the first sentence. Exactly what is said is down to your own judgement, but there needs to be something which sets the offender's expectations in the right direction.

- **To agree a provisional plan of action** for tackling the clients problems and achieving the jointly agreed (hopefully) goals.

In summary, we:

- Have an assessment interview from which we aim to elicit all the key information from the client about their offending.

- In between the first and second interview, we think about what has been said, clarify what the problems are, what the goals are, and develop a plan to achieve those goals.

- Spend the first five or ten minutes of the second interview explaining to the offender how we see things, explaining how many sessions we are likely to have together and what will happen in them, and generating the person's commitment to this plan. In other words, forming a *contract* between ourselves and the other person.

- Get on with the treatment sessions. So, the first treatment session will (usually) start part of the way through session two. The last treatment session might be a dozen or so sessions later.

3.3D
TREATMENT SESSIONS

Treatment sessions (those after the second meeting) will generally follow the same pattern, namely:

- Check on client's progress since last time

    - but make this fairly brief; the whole session can disappear here if you are not careful.

- Check on last session's homework, if any

    - Having stressed at the end of each session how important the homework task is, it would be undermining to forget to enquire how it went.

- Agree today's agenda - today's Goals and the Plan - with the client

    - You will have thought about this in advance, so you will have a provisional or 'default' agenda in your mind. But discuss and produce an agreed one if possible.

- Tackle that agenda

- Set homework if appropriate

    - The homework will be a logical follow on to what has been tackled in the session. It needs to be both achievable and relevant, and you should do your best to ensure that the client is motivated to complete it.

- Summarise

- Get feedback from client. Especially about any issues he thinks were especially important in the session.

All kept to within the allotted time. If you see clients hourly the allotted time will probably be about 45 minutes. This gives time to write up the notes, and to review the next client's notes.

On the next page you will find a sheet which you may wish to use for keeping yourself on track in each session.

SESSION SHEET *for session on* .... *(date).*

Check-list for before the session:

- Re-read Overview sheet

- Read the notes from the last session, and revise what homework was set

- Form a provisional agenda - The Goals and the Plan - for this session, and fill it in:

Today's Provisional Goals and Plan:

_____

_____

_____

_____

_____

_____

Check-list for during the session:

- Check on client's progress since last time

- Check on last session's homework, if any

- Agree today's agenda - the Goals and the Plan - with the client, if possible

- Tackle that agenda

- Set homework if appropriate

- Summarise

- Get feedback from client

Summary of Today's Session, including any homework tasks and any topics you have in mind for the next session:

_____

_____

_____

_____

_____

_____

3.3E

ENDING THERAPY

There are few hard and fast rules about when and how to end therapy, but you might like to think about the following:

- You will probably tail sessions off gradually by increasing the time interval between them from a week to a fortnight to a month, for example.

- The client will know at least at the penultimate session that 'the next session could be the last'. As the whole of therapy is, hopefully, a collaborative venture, both you and the client may - throughout therapy - have a good idea when the close will come.

- Sometimes the two of you may have achieved all the goals. Other times you may have been only, say, 80% successful or less when you decide that it is time to come to a close. In any event, it is unlikely that there are now absolutely <u>no</u> problems or concerns. This does not *necessarily* suggest that they should continue in therapy, however. It is, as they say, a matter of clinical judgement.

- It is probably a good idea for the client to summarise the lessons learned from the session (possibly as a homework task, possibly jointly with you). This (a) emphasises that improvement was not accidental, and (b) encourages use of the same strategies in the future.

- A review session 6 months or so after the end of intervention is a good idea if possible. The feasibility of this may, however, be determined by the circumstances in which you are seeing the client.

CHAPTER 3.4

THE PRINCIPLES IN PRACTICE: GROUPWORK

INTRODUCTION

All that has been said earlier about the importance of the individual characteristics and personality of the helper or therapist applies equally when working in groups. This assertion is illustrated by a study reported by Yalom and Lieberman (1971) which compared the outcome of (encounter) groups directed by leaders with different theoretical orientations. They were unable to show the superiority of any one of those theoretical orientations, but found some startling effects due to the leadership *style* of particular individuals.

Leaders were observed, rated and grouped into one of seven types: "Aggressive Stimulators", "Love Leaders", "Social Engineers", "Laissez-Faire", "Cool, Aggressive Stimulators", "High Structure" and "The Tape Leaders".

 (UNFAIR) **EXERCISE:**

Just from the titles of the 7 types of leader, which type do you think you would be?

They found that the style of a group leader was the major cause of casualties. The most damaging style, the "Aggressive Stimulator" was described as intrusive and aggressive, with considerable challenging and confronting of group members. They were impatient and authoritarian, insisting on immediate self-disclosure, emotional expression and attitude change. Of the five leaders in this category, all produced casualties except one, the one exception stating that he deviated from his usual style and pulled his punches. <u>The leaders of this type produced nearly half of all the most severe casualties.</u>

Yalom and Lieberman describe one person's experience as follows:

This subject was unequivocal in her evaluation of her group as a destructive experience. Her group, following the model and suggestions of the leader, was an intensely aggressive one which undertook to help this subject, a passive, gentle individual, to "get in touch with" her anger. Although the group attacked her in many ways, including a physical assault by one of the female members, she most of all remembers the leader's attack on her. At one point he cryptically remarked that she "was on the verge of schizophrenia". He would not elaborate on this statement and it echoed ominously within her for many months.

Clearly that kind of approach is a million miles from the collaborative, empirical, gentle and effective one which characterises cognitive work.

This chapter is divided into 5 sections as follows:

3.4A POSSIBLE BENEFITS OF GROUP THERAPY

3.4B GROUP THERAPY: A PARTIAL HISTORY

3.4C RESEARCH ON GROUPS

3.4D SOME VARIETIES OF GROUP

3.4E SOME GENERAL CONCEPTS PARTICULARLY RELEVANT TO THERAPY IN GROUPS

Don't worry, each section is short!

CHAPTER 3.4A

POSSIBLE BENEFITS OF GROUP THERAPY

While a group approach clearly has some possible drawbacks, especially in terms of assembling the right number of people together at a convenient time for all, finding a suitable location, and so forth, it also has some distinct advantages. Many of these are summarised by Yalom (1975) as follows:

1.   The knowledge that you are not the only person with a particular problem; other people have similar problems. ("Commonality").

2.   A feeling of belonging. This assumes that a sense of cohesiveness is established in a group and that this "belonging-ness" is therefore fostered.

3.   A sense of family membership produced by the sometimes rather family-like relationships that can be established in a group. This can be directly helpful when group members are concerned about relating to parents, partners, children.

4.   The ability to ventilate feelings which have previously been kept to oneself. Often referred to as catharsis.

5.   Straightforward information can be given about particular problems and their resolutions. The fact that this information is heard by several people simultaneously plainly increases the cost-effectiveness of the leader.

6.   Hope may be produced by feeling that something is being done to help ones problem.

7.   The feeling of altruism which people experience in helping each other may result in individual feeling better about themselves.

8.   Social skills may develop thanks to (a) practice in interacting with others and (b) direct feedback obtained from other members of the group.

9.   Modelling. An individual may copy the behaviour or coping strategies of other people in the group, possibly including the leader.

One might add to that the following:

1. **Cognitive self-challenging.** Given support and questioning from a group, individuals may talk through a particular issue and challenge themselves about thoughts and feelings they have been experiencing. This may lead to them acting quite differently - and hopefully better - than previously.

2. **Problem Solving.** Individuals in a group may go through the traditional stages of problem solving. Clearly describing a problem - generating possible solutions (or having them proposed by other group members) - weighing up the pros and cons of each solution (often with the help from other group members) - taking a decision as to which course to follow.

3. **Homework.** Group members may set themselves tasks to do before the next group meeting (and indeed the group leader, or others, may prompt an individual to do so). Many people view such homework tasks as important for transferring knowledge and insight gained in the group to "real life".

4. It is also perhaps worth noting that the 'commonality' referred to by Yalom in 1 above is not always an advantage. Just as many depressed people find that being in a group of other depressed people is far from advantageous, so many group leaders report that some offenders may confirm each others' maladaptive attitudes and ways of seeing life. This suggests that great care should be taken in the composition of the group.

 EXERCISE:

Read through the above benefits of group therapy and place a tick by those you think would apply when working with offenders. (Yalom was talking about the benefits of a group approach *in general*, rather than specifically applied to offenders.) Place a double-tick by any you consider *especially* relevant.

Are there any additional advantages you can think of?

_____

_____

EXERCISE

Below are listed the cognitive techniques we discussed in Module Two. Which of them do you think could be taught to a **group** of offenders?

(Tick)

- Methods of *identifying* automatic thoughts.

- Methods of *changing* automatic thoughts.

- Methods of identifying beliefs and rules, and methods of changing them.

- Positive Self-Talk; establishing positive perceptions rather than simply eliminating negative ones.

- Benson's cognitive relaxation method.

- Helping clients to schedule specific activities through the week.

- Record-Keeping: recording the week's activities.

- Distraction.

CHAPTER 3.4B

GROUP THERAPY: A PARTIAL HISTORY

Some people think of group work as being rather 'groupie', as though in some way that is difficult to define, it is all linked up with free love, faded jeans and rigidly-liberal views. This is not necessarily the case, and while it may sound rather appealing, not all group leaders are like this. Just for the sake of completeness here is an abbreviated history of the group approach:

1.   Joseph Hersey Pratt (1872-1956) was holding weekly group meeting with his tuberculous patients as early as 1905. Pratt was a physician and a large part of the purpose of these meetings was to ensure that patients were adhering to their medical instructions, as well as to enable Pratt to monitor their progress. However, Pratt found that these meetings resulted in patients encouraging each other, feeling less isolated and alone, and therefore becoming less depressed than was usually the case. (Yalom 1985).

2.   Psychodrama came to the United States in the 1920's. Jacob L. Moreno (1890-1974) is normally credited with its introduction there. Moreno (1953) described its purpose as to explore interpersonal relations and private worlds, by means of dramatic techniques.

Moreno had established the theatre of spontaneity in Vienna, where participants in the psychodrama group acted out their problem on a stage in front of an audience. Typically, troublesome feelings experienced by one member of a group would be acted out by one or more other members of the group. The intention was that this should provide insight to the troubled individual.

Nowadays psychodrama is still utilized, although there is not normally an outside audience present. The group members themselves are normally viewed as sufficient. Sometimes videotapes are made of the sessions so that participants can observe their contributions or re-view particular sections which helped them.

3.   S.R.Slavson (1891-1981) ran a group therapy programme at the Jewish Board of Guardians in New York City. This was for disturbed children and adolescents, and Slavson used Freudian psychoanalysis in working with these groups.

4.   World War II provided an impetus for group therapy because, by this time, "shell shock" and other post trauma disorders were becoming more widely recognised and accepted, yet the number of therapists was still very limited. Group

therapy was therefore viewed as one means of offering therapy to as wide a population as possible. Basically such therapy tended to be individual therapy, but applied to a group of people at a time. Indeed this is still probably the most widely used approach, and most methods of individual psychotherapy have been utilized in groups.

5.   The T-Group was originally conceived in 1947, by colleagues of Kurt Lewin. Their purpose was to increase the efficiency of businessmen by making them more conscious of their effect on other people and their own feelings about others. The T-Group was, and is, an educational and personal-development group, rather than being intended for disturbed individuals.

6.   Encounter Groups became very popular in the 1960's, particularly in the West Coast of America, especially at the Esalen Institute where Perls was in residence. Encounter Groups were similar in purpose to T-Groups but made extensive use of physical contact and touching exercise, as well as the verbal interactions favoured by T-Groups. Rogers (1970) says that T-Groups and Encounter Groups are usually impossible to distinguish from each other nowadays.

7.   It is probably true that in the U.K. in the 1990's the most common groups are basically delivering individual psychotherapy to several people at a time. As Costello and Costello (1992) put it "group therapy is the assembling of a group of people with psychological problems for the purpose of discussing their problems under the guidance of a professional trained leader ... (It) can take a variety of specific forms determined principally by the theoretical perspective of the leader and the kinds of problems the participants bring.

8.   In spite of the above, it is nevertheless true that therapy in group provides processes and opportunities which are not available in individual therapy, just as the reverse is also the case.

EXERCISE

Put the jeans away.

CHAPTER 3.4C

RESEARCH ON GROUPS

Research on groups in relatively poor. Kaul and Bednar (1986) reviewed 477 articles published between 1977 and 1983 and viewed only 17 as worthy of discussion. The following is based on their review.

1.   Group Therapies of different kinds appear to have generally beneficial effects on a wide range of clients. In some instances these effects have been sustained and followed up after several months.

2.   Dependent people seem to do better in highly structured groups, whereas independent better-functioning individuals improved more in less structured ones, where they can express themselves more easily.

3.   There are no particular advantages in "marathon groups" - those that sustained themselves over an entire weekend with minimal breaks for absolute essentials.

4.   People who become worse during the course of treatment - "Casualties" - are relatively few, less than 3% in most studies. However, this is perhaps due to careful screening and conscientious monitoring of the group.

Additionally:

5.   There is evidence that behavioural and cognitive-behavioural groups are particular effective (Rose 1986).

6.   It would appear that cohesive groups may produce better results for their members than less cohesive ones. Possibly this is because it enables participants to talk more openly about their feelings and problems, and thereby open themselves up to resolving their feelings and solving their problems. (Budman et al 1987).

7.   It would appear that the feedback in groups is important, especially if negative feedback is accompanied by positive feedback additionally. (Jacobs et al 1973).

EXERCISE

Place a tick or double-tick by those findings above which seem especially relevant to cognitive group-work with offenders.

CHAPTER 3.4D

SOME VARIETIES OF GROUP

Costello and Costello (1992) defined group therapy as "... the assembling of a group of people with psychological problems for the purpose of discussing their problems under the guidance of a professionally trained leader ... (It) can take a variety of specific forms determined principally by the theoretical perspective of the leader and the kinds of problems the participants bring."

That is probably the most realistic conceptualisation of group therapy in the U.K. in the 1990's. Nevertheless, there are distinctions made between various types of group, though how "pure" these distinctions are in reality is debatable. For the sake of completeness, the following are some of the distinctions made.

1.   *Behaviour therapy groups*. Described particularly by Arnold Lazarus (1968) such groups may, for example, implement a systematic desensitization programme to several people simultaneously.

2.   *Social Skills Training Groups*. These are now widespread and are possibly one of the "purest" groups currently employed.

3.   *Assertion Training Groups*. Considered by some to be a sub-species of social skills training.

4.   *Problem-Solving Groups*. Described for example by Rose (1986).

5.   *Insight Orientated Groups*. Specifically T-Groups and Encounter Groups, aimed at "sensitivity training".

Some broader distinctions are made as follows:

1.   There is a distinction between groups where the therapist is predominantly conducting individual therapy with each of the members present (although there is of course vicarious learning, and the therapist can utilize group processes for each of the members) and groups where all the interactions between individuals are regarded equally (and one might therefore regard it as having a facilitator, but no real "leader").

2.   Conjoint therapy for couples.

3.   Family therapy.

4.   Groups that have a fixed membership, versus groups that have a fluid membership.

5.   Groups that run for a specific length of time (say 12 sessions) versus groups that run indeterminately.

6.   Self Help Groups, such as Alcoholic Anonymous, Weight Watchers, Cruse, Clubs for Single Parents, Clubs for People with Handicapped Children, etc.

 KEY EXERCISE

What are the defining characteristics of the group(s) that you run or intend to run? Specifically:

How many members would it have?

_____

Would membership be 'fixed' or 'fluid'

_____

How many sessions would a group last for?

_____

How would you encourage members to keep attending?

_____

Would group members all have been convicted of similar offences?

_____

If so, are there any advantages or disadvantages of this?

_____

These last two questions are especially important ones. Take the following scenarios from outside of the forensic arena: If you put a group of anxious people together each person is reassured that he is not so inadequate after all, there are plenty of others just the same; what is more other people are not really that threatening, in fact many are just like him. In fact, the very act of putting anxious people in a group is sometimes the major therapeutic effect. On the other hand, if you put a group of depressed people together, the reverse is the case. Each person already has a negative view of themselves and of others, and both of these are reinforced by being in a group of others in a similar situation.

Which of these scenarios does your planned group match more closely?

CHAPTER 3.4E

SOME GENERAL CONCEPTS PARTICULARLY RELEVANT TO THERAPY IN GROUPS

The following observations are just as relevant when adopting a cognitive approach with *individuals*. Nevertheless, they probably bear repeating:

1. It is usually beneficial to **focus on goals** which the individual particular wants to achieve, rather than attempting to "totally reconstruct" the individual.

2. **Counselling-type skills** such as empathy, warmth, genuineness and unconditional positive regard appear to have just as wide an application as in the pure counselling setting.

3. Emphasis on the **"here and now"** is often more effective than diverging onto the more historical perspective.

4. It may be useful to capitalize on insights developed during a group session by having the participant(s) develop **plans and homework** tasks to do outside of the groups.

5. **The monitoring of progress** and evaluation of what is happening is always important, especially outside of the group sessions when one can think about things "coolly" and possibly discuss with a colleague.

A final comment:

Some people feel that if they put someone in a group then they are disallowed from seeing them individually. Not so; there is no law against doing both over the same period of time.

COGNITIVE SELF-TEST, MODULE 3.

Again, there is no need to write anything, just read the questions and compose mental answers. Check back to the text if you wish.

1
In the study by Crits-Christoph et al (cited by Lambert 1989) which was found to be more important, the techniques a therapist used or the therapist's personal characteristics?

2
Ricks (1974) compared two therapists, 'supershrink' and 'pseudoshrink' and found that one was greatly more effective than the other. What were the main differences between the two therapists?

3
What skills and personal qualities were described as being important for the successful implementation of a cognitive approach? (pp75-77)

4
On page 79, we discuss the relationship between the professional and the offender. What are the three levels of the relationship that we should consider. What is the 'deepest' level?

5
We described page 80 as 'one of the most important pages in the entire book. Why? What is it that gives rise to our beliefs / rules and our automatic thoughts?

6
What is the aim of the first interview with an offender?

7
Part of the assessment interview includes looking at the offender's childhood and schooling. Why do you suppose this is important? (if you are stuck, see Module 1, p18-21).

8
And what should you hope to achieve in the second interview?

9
Page 93 details the plan for a typical session involving a cognitive approach. Although you can refer back, it should become engraved firmly on the mind. What is it?

10
When you are working towards the end of contact with an offender, maybe at the last or the penultimate session, you should ask him to summarise the lessons learned during therapy. Why?

11
Yalom and Lieberman compared the outcome of encounter groups directed by leaders of different styles and found that 'aggressive stimulators' had by far the worst outcome. How were aggressive stimulators described? (p96).

12
Having read this module, what would you say are the main advantages of adopting a cognitive approach with a *group* of offenders rather than with individuals? And the main disadvantages?

13
World War II provided a boost for group therapy because of (the numbers of potential clients and) the prevalence of shell-shock and other post-trauma complaints. Why would a group approach be especially relevant to these? (If stuck, see p105, final para.)

14
According to Budman et al which groups generally work better, cohesive groups or less cohesive groups?

15
If you were to run a group employing a cognitive approach to help offenders, how many people would you have in it, and what offences would they have committed? Why?

16.
One of the themes of this module is that a *collaborative* approach from the professional is very important indeed (see, for example page 76), but can be difficult with some offenders. How easy or difficult do you anticipate *you* would find this?

MODULE FOUR:

THE BROADER PERSPECTIVE

AIMS

To put a cognitive approach into a broader perspective by briefly covering some of the other factors which are relevant to treating serious offending. Specifically:

- Biological factors such as exercise, nutrition, drug effects and sleep.

- Environmental factors.

- Social factors.

CHAPTER 4.1

THE RELEVANT BIOLOGICAL FACTORS

Aerobic exercise

Persuading clients to exercise is one of the most difficult tasks that a therapist has. This is unfortunate, for a number of papers over many years have pointed to substantial beneficial effects on clients both in terms of alleviating depression and anxiety, and hence irritability and anger. The key component appears to be that the exercise takes an aerobic form. In other words, exercises such as walking, running, sustained swimming, cycling, rowing. There are other specialised aerobic exercises such as aerobic dance, which are usually performed in classes. The same thing would apply to "stepping", a recent addition. *Anaerobic* exercises include sprinting, tennis, football, volleyball, golf.

The summary of rules and tips for exercising:

- Build exercise into your routine and don't allow other factors to interfere with that routine.

- Make progress slowly. Any exercise is better than no exercise at all.

- Aim for twenty minutes aerobic exercise per day. Something like purposeful walking is very good indeed.

- People usually enjoy their exercise more if it contains variety. For example, whilst most days might be walking, some days might be swimming.

- Wear clothes which make exercising easy. For example, some people could do their twenty minutes walking on the way back from work, but are prevented from doing so by unsuitable clothes or shoes.

In general, twenty minutes aerobic exercise, every other day, is probably sufficient. In practice, most people have difficulty in sustaining 'every other day' as part of their routine, and may in fact find it easier to exercise *every* day. This is simply because it more easily becomes a matter of routine. This 'routine' aspect is an important one which helps people to sustain the habit. To assist with this, people should be encouraged to put aside specific times during the day for their exercise and not to allow other factors to interfere with that set time.

People should be encouraged to make progress slowly, any exercise is better than no exercise at all and it is surprising just how low-level exercise can be to benefit the person. Twenty minutes purposeful walking is fine.

Benefits of aerobic exercise include:

- Improved sleep

- Increased self-esteem

- Decrease in feelings of stress and depression

- Increased stamina

- Weight loss (if calorie intake held constant)

- Increased life expectancy

- Decrease in probability of coronary heart disease

- Increased total blood volume

- Decreased resting pulse

- Increased skeleton muscle volume

- Increased number of capillaries

It is the first 3 on this list which are of particular relevance for some offenders, because of their link with irritability and anger, and therefore some aggressive offences.

It is a curious fact that in order to be sure of obtaining enough exercise in the UK one either has to be a dog or detained in one of Her Majesty's Prisons. If in the latter, you can be assured of one hour's exercise every day, which is probably more than most un-detained people have. Dog owners who see their pets looking 'down in the mouth' immediately seek to remedy it by ensuring their pet has sufficient exercise, and maybe purchasing a vitamin supplement.

Nutrition ○

While it is certainly true that most Western countries consume a more than ample amount of nutrients, it is equally true that some individuals in those countries do not. In a recent study described by Jacobson, 5% of people attending their physician in America complaining of fatigue were diagnosed as suffering from insufficient nutrition.

In that study it was hypothesized that the main reason for the lack of nutrition was financial. Equally, however, one meets people who - even though they have the financial resources - simply do not feed themselves properly, either through apathy or through consuming their calories through alcohol rather than food.

Guidelines on nutrition are notorious for their variation over the years. It is probably safe to say that most people who are eating anything like 'normal' are receiving sufficient nutrition. However, it is worth asking people just what they do habitually eat, working through the day in a systematic fashion. If in doubt, there seems to be no harm in suggesting that they might purchase a vitamin and mineral supplement which are widely available and cost in the region of 10p per day, possibly less. However, these supplements should really be regarded as safety nets, rather than a realistic alternative to proper nutrition. (There is also some evidence that, *unless one is specifically diagnosed as suffering from anaemia,* one of probably best to steer clear of supplementary iron, an excess of which - some authorities maintain - is linked to heart disease.)

A vitamin supplement is especially advisable for people who drink alcohol excessively, because alcohol depletes the body's store of B-vitamins. These are instrumental in looking after our 'nerves', meaning that a significant lowering of B-vitamin levels may lead to anxiety, depression and irritability. As mentioned earlier this may predispose the person to more aggression – both in domestic and outside situations – than would otherwise be the case.

It may also be worth asking about the *timing* of meals. It probably does not matter especially what time meals are taken, so long as a degree of *regularity* is maintained.

Drugs

Predominantly Unhelpful Drugs:
The three drugs most commonly used are caffeine, alcohol and tobacco. All have their problems, alcohol because it inhibits the storage of important vitamins, tobacco because (apart from the hugely decreased life expectancy associated with smoking) it is the most common cause of low level carbon monoxide intake. All because they work against effective sleep.

A table illustrating the caffeine content of some drinks and foods:

	Average Caffeine Content (milligrams)
Coffee (5 oz cup)	
brewed drip method	115
brewed percolator	80
instant	65
decaffeinated, brewed	3
decaffeinated, instant	2
Tea (5 oz cup)	
brewed	50
instant	30
iced (12 oz glass)	70
Cocoa beverage (5 oz cup)	4
Chocolate milk beverage (8 oz)	5
Milk Chocolate (1 oz)	6
Dark Chocolate, semi-sweet (1 oz)	20
Coca Cola (12 oz)	45.6
Diet Coke	45.6
Pepsi Cola	38.4
Diet Pepsi	36
Pepsi Light	36

Some weight control aids, alertness tablets and dueretics also contain significant amounts of caffeine.

Source: US Food and Drugs Administration.

Although some people find that alcohol relaxes them and they will fall asleep more easily, others find the reverse. For just about everybody, alcohol consumption late in the evening produces a disturbed night's sleep. In some people it can trigger or aggravate sleep apnea (episodes where the sleeper stops breathing).

Once a heavy drinker stops drinking, an improvement can occur as quickly as two weeks later. However it can take much longer, and in some people sleep is still disturbed two years later.

It is important, of course, not to mix alcohol and sleeping pills. This is sometimes a danger because people who have troubled sleep will try anything, but the combination can lead to serious side effects.

As far as smoking is concerned, a smoker will have something like eight times the amount of carbon monoxide in the blood compared with someone in a rural environment, and about twice the amount of someone in a city centre environment. The long term effect of this can be to decrease energy levels.

The decrease in energy level is of course counteracted by the nicotine in cigarettes which is a stimulant and is therefore inclined to keep the person awake. Hauri reports that insomnia "ranks near the top of complaints expressed by smokers". Hardly surprising, perhaps, since cigarettes raise blood pressure, speed up the heart rate, and stimulate brain-wave activity. Hauri also suggests that the fact that many smokers tend to wake up more in the middle of the night is possibly explained by the body experiencing withdrawal symptoms.

It is also important to ask about caffeine intake because of its importance (a) in possibly impairing sleep, and (b) because it can exacerbate symptoms of agitation. As can be seen from the table above, the major sources of caffeine are: coffee (fresh-brewed or instant); tea (to some people's surprise); Cola drinks (including their Diet versions); and, to a lesser extent, chocolate (though not drinking chocolate).

Sleep

Sleep is a self-evidently important aspect in treating agitated, irritable and sometimes aggressive people. On the one hand, impaired sleep is rightly regarded as a symptom both of depression and anxiety, on the other hand the very fact of having impaired sleep exacerbates both conditions. People who do not sleep well tend to suffer impaired mood during the day-time as a result, and also have extra time at night when they can dwell, brood or become agitated about life events.

Strictly speaking, impaired sleep should be tackled very systematically using a sleep diary and steadily varying key factors. However the following is offered as a list of some key measures to increase the chances of a good night's sleep.

- Make every attempt to reduce caffeine intake, particularly after 2pm.

- Try to limit alcohol consumption, particularly later on in the evening.

- Try to cut down on or cut out cigarettes.

- Learn and use a good relaxation technique, both for a 'pure relaxation' session during the day, and to control your all day stress levels.

- Take time to 'wind down' before going to bed and trying to sleep; slumping into bed exhausted does not usually lead to a solid night's sleep.

- Enjoy being relaxed in bed; avoid "trying to sleep".

- Set a routine for yourself, going to bed at regular times and getting up at regular times.

- Take regular exercise, but not within two hours of going to bed.

- Eat a reasonably normal healthy diet, but don't overeat late at night, nor starve yourself before going to bed.

- Try to avoid sleeping pills, which tend to work only for a short time and may lead to 'rebound insomnia'.

- Check that your bed is reasonably comfortable; some people can sleep on hard boards, but they are exceptional. It is true that your partner's restlessness also interferes with your own sleep, especially if you have an unsophisticated bed.

- Try to eliminate sudden sharp noises during the night and eliminate most light; humans tend to sleep better in the dark.

- Set the room to encourage sleep; for example if you clock-watch when awake, don't have the clock staring you in the face by the bed.

There are also a number of misconceptions regarding sleep. Some people are adamant in their belief that a "normal" adult requires, say, 8 hours sleep per night, or 7 hours, or whatever figure. The fact is that people vary tremendously: whereas some adults only need 4 hours per night, others are sleep-deficient on twice that amount. Equally, some people focus only on the length of sleep rather than the quality of it. In fact the *efficiency* of one's sleep is a key concept, the idea that one seeks to be refreshed by sleep, rather than simply spending a long time 'unconscious'.

Further, the fear of not sleeping undermines some people, who can lie awake at night worrying about how their sleeplessness will impair their performance the next day, which in turn makes it difficult for them to get to sleep. In fact, performance on specific tasks is remarkably unhampered by lack of sleep, even though one's mood is. Having said that of course, tiredness causes a number of accidents simply through individuals going to sleep for example in motorway driving.

CHAPTER 4.2

THE ENVIRONMENT

Although many people in the helping professions are used to looking at relatively sophisticated processes, there are sometimes quite gross environmental factors which also need addressing. Some professionals believe that this is outside of their remit, and while this may or not be the case it is certainly true that some environmental factors have to be addressed by someone, if not by us, then by somebody else. In any event we need to be aware of them, and to ensure that these factors are addressed.

Such environmental factors tend to be idiosyncratic - specific to the individual - so teasing them out involves getting a feel for what is going on in a person's life. However, the following are some examples:

1. **Financial matters** sometimes weigh heavily on people and can cause a high degree of - realistic - agitation. If a person is in fear of eviction, having their house repossessed or being made bankrupt, the finer points of their thinking style, for example, can appear somewhat irrelevant to them. Whilst we, as therapists, may not be experts in financial matters, we can sometimes give support while the client works out what their best plan of action is, and indeed while they carry it out.

2. Some people manage to produce a dramatic misfit between themselves and their **chosen occupation**. Although the way we view things is important, it is also useful to examine the *fit* between person and occupation. 'Occupation' is not necessarily the same as 'job': one woman was severely worried, concerned and depressed partly because of a voluntary activity she became involved with. Initially it was exciting and productive and involved close team-work with a number of other volunteers. Gradually the others lost interest, over a period of two years or more. This left her as the only person involved, with considerable responsibility and little support. Additionally she was beginning to alienate other friends by seeking involvement from them. Relinquishing involvement in this project and replacing it with a more rewarding activity (in this case a two-year educational course) proved to be very beneficial for her. **Unemployment** is also an issue which sometimes needs extended consideration.

3. **Where people live** sometimes appears to be influential. The influence of 'poor housing' is obvious, and may or may not lend itself to improvement. Sharing a house with relatives can be a major issue, and interacts with social issues, considered later. It is also the case however, that one sees people who have simply chosen somewhere to live that suits them very badly, either because of

the location, the neighbours, or some indefinable aspect. One man I saw craved close contact with the sea, and his wife had unwittingly carried out a very skilled A-B-A experimental design with him: before they were married he was a cheerful soul who captained a cargo-carrying steamer; when they became married he obtained a job in a factory and settled into long term morose-ness; when they agreed he should return to sea - this time on an oil rig - he regained his former cheerfulness, even in the two-week stretches back home. (His particular problems arose when an explosion on the oil rig meant that he became phobic of such conditions, and - back on dry land again - his former morose-ness returned.)

4. Sometimes, **a key object in the environment** is a relatively simple, tangible one which could - and perhaps should have been - altered very easily. For example one person had a large, thirsty, unreliable car, with the obvious result that there was always a degree of uncertainty as to whether he would reach his destination, and this was sometimes important to his job. Even when the car did not let him down, it consumed a lot of petrol which also preyed on his mind. Trading it in for a smaller, reliable model produced a significant reduction in agitation out of proportion to the complexity of the act.

CHAPTER 4.3

SOCIAL ASPECTS

Interpersonal therapy (IPT) has shown itself to be a remarkably effective therapy in some US studies (Klerman et al). It is a time limited therapy predominantly aimed at people who are depressed. Harry Stack-Sullivan maintained however that psychiatry is the study of the person's relationships, and it is easy to see that these are relevant to offending. This is especially so given that a high proportion of major violent incidents take place within the home. The core aspect of IPT is that it focuses on the person's relationships and endeavours to enhance these.

Klerman et al suggest that relationship difficulties normally fall under one of four headings, as follows:

1. **Grief.** On-going or unresolved grief plainly can have a tremendous negative affect on people. Sometimes it is very difficult indeed to help clients resolve their grief, but even in those cases it may be possible to resolve associated problems such as anger and guilt. *Occasionally* it is possible to enable the client to totally re-frame what has happened, so that they may eventually re-interpret a 'loss' as 'at least we had five happy years together'. At other times such re-framing is simply not achievable.

2. **Role-disputes.** These normally take the form of disputes between partners who are living together and may benefit from being resolved in one way or another, either by some form of compromise or agreement, or by separating.

3. **Change in role.** There are numerous changes in role which people can have trouble adapting to. For example, from son/daughter to partner; from parent of dependent children to parent of independent children who have left home; from partner to separated / divorced / widowed person; from work-mate to supervisor. And many more.

4. **Social isolation.** It seems that most humans are basically sociable beings and becoming isolated can lead to problems. Social isolation does not always occur through lack of social skill, sometimes it is through unrealistic social anxiety, other times through simple lack of sufficient effort in a social direction. Klerman et al make the point that it is sometimes not so much the actual degree of isolation as how satisfactory the client views their social circle, particularly at times of crisis. Some clients say - or imply - that their friends would 'run a mile' if they started talking about personal matters. Unfortunately, in some instances, they are absolutely right. On other occasions people can be pleasantly

surprised at the support they can receive if only they can bring themselves to start talking about the matters that are of concern to them.

The nature of the conversation that clients have with their friends is also a major factor. Some will indulge in the 'Ain't It Awful' game, where the friend simply agrees and develops the client's theme on the awfulness of life / their boss / their partner. This usually has the effect of aggravating the situation rather than improving it. Clients who involve themselves in constructive conversations about their problems sometimes establish a firm, long-lasting and effective source of support. Occasionally, the conversations they have with us, the therapists, can serve as a good model for conversations elsewhere, especially if we are following Burnard's advice to 'be a friend, not a therapist'.

WELL, THAT'S IT ...

... you have done it. I hope it was reasonably painless. I also hope you have managed to make sense of it in terms of the way you like to work, and the constraints you are under. It is difficult to summarise all we have discussed, but how about this:

1. Develop a good relationship with the client.
2. Remember the session plan (How have things been since last time; How was the homework; What shall we talk about today, I suggest ...; Get on and talk about it; Set homework; Summarise; Obtain feedback). This is so even if you are working with groups.
3. Get the person's life in order, as far as possible, generally. Remember it is no use talking about the finer points of a person's cognitions if they never have a decent night's sleep, have turned night into day and day into night, or whatever.
4. Fill in the cognitive model (Early experience; Dysfunctional beliefs and rules; Key incident; Negative automatic thoughts; Response). Don't be tempted to skimp, it really helps us to see what is going on.
5. Use the good relationship you have with the client (and some techniques in Module Two) to work towards producing desirable change.

Good luck! And do let me know how you get on in applying a cognitive approach to your work, and what you think of this book if you get the chance!

William Davies, APT.

REFERENCES:

(**Bold** indicates key texts for further reading if required.)

COGNITIVE THERAPY

Adler, A. (1919). *Problems of Neurosis.* Kegan Paul, London.

Bandura, A. (1969). *Principles of Behaviour Modification.* Holt, Rhinehart and Wilson, New York.

Beck, A.T. (1963). Thinking and Depression. I. Idiosyncratic content and cognitive distortions. *Archives of General Psychiatry,* 9, 324-333.

Beck, A.T. (1976) *Cognitive Therapy and the Emotional Disorders.* Penguin.

Beck, A.T., Rush, A.J., Shaw, B.F. and Emery, G. (1979). *Cognitive Therapy of Depression.* The Guilford Press, New York.

Beck, A.T. & Emery, G. (1985). *Anxiety Disorder and Phobias: a Cognitive Perspective.* Basic Books, New York.

Blackburn, I. and Davidson, K. (1990). *Cognitive Therapy For Depression & Anxiety.* Blackwell, Oxford.

Crits-Christoph, P., Luborsky, L., McLellan, A.T., Woody, G., Piper, W., Lieberman, B. & Imber, S. *Do psychotherapists vary much in their success? The answer within four outcome studies.*

Ellis, A. (1962). *Reason and Emotion in Psychotherapy.* Lyle Stuart, New York.

Goleman, D. (1985, August 2nd). Switching therapists may be best. Indianapolis News, p9.

Hawton, K., Salkovskis, P.M., Kirk, J. and Clark, D.M. (1989). *Cognitive Behaviour Therapy for Psychiatric Problems: A Practical Guide.* Oxford University Press, Oxford.

Kelly, G.A. (1955). *The Psychology of Personal Constructs.* Norton, New York.

Lambert, M.J. (1989). The psychotherapist's contribution to psychotherapy process and outcome. Clinical Psychology Review 9: 469-85.

Luborsky, L., McLellan, A.T., Woody, G.E., O'Brien, C.P. & Auerbach, A. (1985). Therapist success and its determinants. *Archives of General Psychiatry,* 42, 602-611

Mahoney, M.J. (1991). *Human Change Processes.* Basic Books, New York.

Miller, N.E. and Dollard, J. (1941). *Social Learning and Imitation.* Yale University Press, New Haven, Connecticut.

Orlinsky, D.E. & Howard, K.I. (1980). Gender and psychotherapeutic outcome. In A.M.Brodksy & R.T.Hare-Mustin (Eds.), *Women and psychotherapy* (pp3-34). New York: Guilford Press.

Ricks, D.F. (1974). Supershrink: Methods of a therapist judged successful on the basis of adult outcomes of adolescent patients. In D.F.Ricks, M.Roff & A.Thomas (Eds.), *Life history research in psychopathology.* Minneapolis: University of Minnesota Press.

Rotter, J.B. (1954). *Social Learning and Clinical Psychology.* Prentice Hall, Englewood Cliffs, New Jersey.

Trower,P., Casey, A. and Dryden, W. (1988). *Cognitive-Behavioural Counselling in Action.* **Sage, London.**

GROUP WORK

(**Bold** indicates key texts for further reading if required.)

Costello, T.W. & Costello, J.T. (1992). *Abnormal Psychology* (2nd Ed). New York, Harper Collins.

Kaul, T.J. & Bedner, R.L. (1986). Experiential Group Research: Results, Questions, and Suggestions. In S.L. Garfield and A.E. Pergin (Eds), *Handbook of Psychotherapy and Behaviour Change* (3rd Ed). New York : Wiley

Lazarus, A.A. (1968). Behaviour Therapy in Groups. In G.M. Gazta (Eds), *Basic Approach to Group Psychotherapy and Counselling.* Springfield, Ill.: Charles C. Thomas.

Rogers, C.R. (1970). *Carl Rogers on Encounter Groups.* New York: Harper and Row.
Yalom, I.D. & Lieberman, M.A. (1971). A study of encounter group casualties. *Archives of General Psychiatry,* 47, 427-439.

Rose, S.D. (1986). Group Methods in F.H. Kanfer and A.P. Goldstein (Eds), *Helping People Change : A Textbook of Methods (3rd Ed.)* Elmsford, N.Y. : Pergaman.

Yalom, I.D. (1985) *The Theory and Practice of Group Psychotherapy* **(3rd Ed). New York : Basic Books.**

THE BROADER PERSPECTIVE

Bowlby, J. 1969. *Attachment and Loss, Volume 1: Attachment.* London: Hogarth Press.

Brown, G.W., Harris, T., and Copeland, J.R. 1977. Depression and Loss. *Brit. J. Psychiat.* 130: 1-18.

Egan, G. (1990). The Skilled Helper (Fourth Edition). Brooks/Cole, Pacific Grove, California.

Elkin, I, et al (1989) National Institute for Mental Health Treatment of Depression Collaborative Research Program. *Arch Gen Psychiatry,* v46, 971-982.

Hauri, P and Linde, S. (1990). *No More Sleepless Nights.* Wiley, New York.

Goffman, E. 1961 *Asylums.* New York, Doubleday.

Henderson, S., Byrne, D.G., and Duncan, P. 1982. *Neurosis and the Social Environment* Sydney: Academic Press.

Klerman, G.L., Weissman, M.M., Rounsaville, B.J. and Chevron, E.S. (1984). *Interpersonal Psychotherapy of Depression.* Basic Books, New York.

Mahoney, M.J. (1974). *Cognition and Behaviour Modification.* Ballinger, Cambridge, Mass.

Meyer, A. 1957. *Psychobiology: A Science of Man.* Springfield, Ill.: Charles C. Thomas.

Rutter, M. 1972. *Maternal Deprivation Reassessed.* London: Penguin Books.

Sullivan, H.S. 1956. *Clinical Studies in Psychiatry.* New York: Norton.

Thorpe, G.L. and Olson, S.L. (1990). *Behaviour Therapy: Concepts, Procedures and Applications.* Allyn and Bacon, Needham Heights, Massachusetts